A Rainbow in the Desert

An Anthology of Early Twentieth-Century Japanese Children's Literature

Yukie Ohta, Translator

Introduction by Joan E. Ericson
Illustrations by Keico Watanabe

An East Gate Book

LONDON AND NEW YORK

An East Gate Book

First published 2001 by M.E. Sharpe

Published 2017 by Routledge
2 Park Square, Milton Park, Abingdon, Oxon OX14 4RN
711 Third Avenue, New York, NY 10017, USA

Routledge is an imprint of the Taylor & Francis Group, an informa business

Library of Congress Cataloging-in-Publication Data

A rainbow in the desert : an anthology of early twentieth century Japanese children's literature / translated by Yukie Ohta.
p. cm.
"An East gate book."
Summary: A collection of Japanese children's literature in translation spans three decades with contributions by major authors as well as familiar lullabies.
ISBN 0-7656-0555-4 (cloth : alk. paper)—ISBN 0-7656-0556-2 (pbk. : alk. paper)
1. Japan–Literary collections. 2. Children's literature, Japanese. [1. Japan—Literary collections. 2. Japanese literature—Collections.] I. Ohta, Yukie, 1969–

PZ5 .R1334 2000
895.6′0809282′09041—dc21 00058837

ISBN 13: 978-0-7656-0556-6 (pbk)

For Alexi

CONTENTS

~ A Play ~

~ Poems ~

INTRODUCTION

Joan E. Ericson

In the early decades of the twentieth century, Japanese children's literature emerged, first, as an immensely popular and, then, strikingly innovative literary genre. A succession of journals dedicated to children's literature proved commercially successful and, in the post-World War I prosperity, a host of major literary figures embraced the movement to produce high-quality literature for children. Yet standard literary histories, both in Japanese and English, neglect these works. Children's literature is virtually segregated from any discussion of broader intellectual or social trends, and the works by the prominent authors in this collection, Arishima Takeo (1878–1923), Shiga Naoya (1883–1971), Kitahara Hakushū (1885–1942), Akutagawa Ryūnosuke (1892–1927), Nakano Shigeharu (1902–1979), Hayashi Fumiko (1903–1951), Dazai Osamu (1909–1948), and Kinoshita Junji (b. 1914–) as well as other writers of adult fiction who also wrote for children, such as Tokuda Shūsei (1871–1943), Shimazaki Tōson (1872–1943), Izumi Kyōka (1873–1939), Yosano Akiko (1878–1942), and Nogami Yaeko (1885–1985), are very rarely, if ever, given any consideration in the critical evaluations of their oeuvre. Ogawa Mimei (1882–1961) and, notably, Miyazawa Kenji (1896–1933) constitute exceptions—writers well-known for their work for children—that underscore the general invisibility of children's literature by major modern authors.

This anthology of Japanese children's literature significantly contributes to the recovery of an important field. These stories, heretofore untranslated or generally unavailable in North America, allow readers access to a range of literary styles and approaches adopted for children.[1] Their contribution is two-fold: the stories represent an important element of Japanese popular culture, one that contains a significant critique of the culture of modernity; and the stories reflect the evolving concept of childhood that was central to the early twentieth century Japanese discourses on motherhood, education and gender. The representations of childhood found in these stories offer a critical zone of engagement for appreciating the literary, intellectual and social history of modern Japan.

Lineages of Children's Literature

Histories of Japanese literature and graphic arts have long identified tales and traditions that, it was presumed, addressed children, principally because of their simplicity, brevity, comic humor or didactic moralizing. The striking satiric illustrations of the *Chōjūgiga* (Animal scrolls) attributed to Kakuyū Toba (1053–1140) that so effectively parodied twelfth century priests and nobles is the best known example of a comic art tradition, often gruesome or grotesque, and unsparing in ridicule. By the eighteenth century, picture books, illustrated monochrome booklets that used colloquial captions or blocks of text, drew on the common currency of fables or folktales from the most celebrated classical literary compilations, including the *Kojiki* (Record of ancient matters, 712 CE) and the *Konjaku monogatari* (Tales of time now past, 1130–1140 CE). However, despite the unparalleled sophistication in graphic arts employed in book illustration and the accessibility of premodern tales for children, the intention of these texts was not, principally, to reach or engage children. Didactic texts of the Tokugawa era *akahon* (red book), used as primers, clearly targeted young readers, but even in these works the emphasis was on the acquisition of literacy and the propagation of state-sanctioned neo-Confucian morality, not in cultivating themes specific to children.[2]

As in the case with contemporary Japanese *manga*—a term coined by the *ukioye* wood-block print artist Hokusai Katsashika (1760–1849)—literary forms associated in the West with children, such as fables or comics, derived from distinct traditions, presumed different audiences, and were consumed in ways that cannot be conflated with Western experience.

Despite the exceptionalism of its lineages, Japanese children's literature developed as part of, and in response to, a global cultural discourse on childhood. The profound rupture in adult literary forms during the Meiji era (1868–1912) was echoed in the rewriting of folktales (*otogibanashi*) as literature for children. The process was anticipated in early Meiji in the misrepresentation by European scholars and residents of Japan of classical fables and tale literature (*setsuwa bungaku*) as having been written for children.[3] However, among scholars in Japan, the emergence of children's literature is identified not with Western representations of Japanese traditions, but with the subsequent practice of revising folktales and fables to address the modern children of the Meiji era.[4]

The first widely recognized modern work of children's literature was Iwaya Sazanami's (1870–1933) *Koganemaru* (1891), a tale about a filial dog. Though the subject was a familiar theme in folktales, the style was a striking departure: entertaining, engaging, and written in a playfully colloquial voice accessible to children, it has been characterized as capturing the imagination of childhood. Iwaya followed with a succession of commercially successful folktale collections. Though the sources of Iwaya's folktales have yet to be identified, one theory holds that many of his tales were taken from an English translation of Japanese folklore compiled in1887 by James Curtis Hepburn (whom we remember for his romanization system), T.H. James, Basil Hall Chamberlain and David Thompson.[5] Whatever the provenance of Iwaya's material, the proliferation of books and journals offering folktales targeted at children in the succeeding decades, while consciously modeled Western children's literature, often including translations of Western classics—for example, Cinderella or Peter Pan—along with the Japanese stories, purported to recapture an embedded national ethos.

The Japanese embrace of folktales as both emblematic of cultural identity and fundamental for the construction, through children, of national citizens reflects many similarities with the Brothers Grimm and nineteenth century German nationalism. Meiji educators championed the morals and ethics embedded in retold folktales, while writers and publishers celebrated the popularity and effectiveness of the tales, stripped of the extraneous through countless retellings, conveying what they argued was the "essence" of literature. Folktales, retold as children's literature, prefigured the late Meiji revalorization of communal customs and rural social relations—what Carol Gluck chronicled as the adoption of an "agrarian myth" in the wake of the Russo-Japanese war of 1904–1905.[6]

By the turn of the century, the popularity of folktale children's literature supported the emergence of specialized monthly journals, produced by commercial publishing houses, with multi-color covers, quality print, extensive advertisement space, aggressive marketing strategies, and sophisticated management. In 1900, the first journal catering specifically to children, *Yōnen sekai* (Child's world), and shortly thereafter, in 1902, the first gender-specific children's magazines, *Shōnenkai* (Boy's world) and *Shōjokai* (Girl's world) developed the format of lavishly illustrated stories and, eventually, serialized comics that would characterize the mass-circulation, thick (up to four hundred pages) monthlies through the 1930s. From 1911, Tachikawa bunko publishing company specialized in cheap editions featuring ninjas and other heroic characters derived from the *kōdan* (storytelling) tradition. Increasing state-censorship from the late1920s prompted an expansion of serialized comics, considered a safer genre, within the monthlies, and the compilation of complete stories as separate, high-quality, high-priced volumes[7]—in contrast to the cheap, mass-circulation *manga* that would dominate the postwar market.

A Literary Movement

The commercial success of the publishing niche for retold folktales precipitated a reaction during the Taishō era (1912–1926), principally by members of the *bundan* (literary establishment), that produced the most distinctive and celebrated children's literature in modern Japan. In August 1912, a group of male, elite, mostly university-educated literati, who were members of Natsume Sōseki's Thursday Club (Mokuyōkai), formed the *Shōnen bungaku kenkūykai* (Youth literature study group), conveying new-found legitimacy to writing for children. Members of this professional association helped to pioneer a striking new style of children's literature in the next decade—a style well represented in this anthology—by adopting altogether new objectives that consciously sought to elevate literary quality, support innovative or individualistic perspectives, and experiment with language and exotic imagery. Moreover, this new style, what would be termed *dōwa* (children's stories), tended to be written by prominent authors of contemporary adult fiction or poetry.

The shift in the character of children's literature in the Taishō era was characterized by the composition of original tales, employing contemporary, often polite language (*degozaimasu*), little dialect, avoiding saccharine affectation, rarely set in the mythic past (no "once upon a time"), often lacking happy endings, with a matter of fact tone, despite occasional phantasmagorical descriptions, and often reflecting Buddhist assumptions of impermanence. Yet the new style also clearly resonated with the new liberalism of Taishō democracy, with contending, sometimes experimental, educational philosophies, and with the relative prosperity that sustained such journals as *Akai tori* (Red bird), the high-cost, high-quality flagship of what is termed the "golden age" of Japanese children's literature.

The new style children's stories presumed a grounding in literary romanticism, and championed *jun bungaku* (pure literature) that would allow the exploration of individual emotions without stereotypic or self-consciously child-like perspectives. The distinction between pure (*jun*) and popular (*taishū*) children's literature in the late 1910s anticipated the principal conceptual antinomies of literary criticism for adult literature in the mid-1920s, between the "pure" confessional fiction (*shishōsetsu*, or I-novel) and the "popular" proletarian literature. Curiously, at the same time that the literary establishment (*bundan*) lost its control over adult fiction, largely due to the proliferation of outlets for publication and income through popular journals, children's literature was recaptured by the literati. A coterie centered around Ogawa Mimei succeeded in promulgating new standards in children's stories, principally through the critical success of the journal *Akai tori*.

Mimei (as he is generally known in Japanese histories) edited an influential single issue journal *Shōnen bunko* (Youth library) in 1906, the year of his graduation from Waseda University, and published his book *Akai fune* (Red boat) four years later. Mimei's distinctive objectives for children's stories, set down in a retrospective essay, recalled his contact with farmers during the summer vacations of his youth; already he could perceive how elements of modernity and the pervasive commodification of everything under capitalism had inexorably altered bucolic farm life and bankrupted the environment.[8] His choice to write only children's literature was motivated, he wrote, by a desire to recapture lost innocence and simplicity, embodied by pre-modern customs, when childhood was both natural and indistinguishable from nature. In *Akai tori*, Mimei explained that "Children's stories (*dōwa*) are not meant for children alone, they are meant for all who have not lost the heart of a child (*kodomo no kokoro*)." In 1923, the poet Kitahara Hakushū echoed Mimei's sentiment, advocating a "return to the child's heart . . . return not just to the innocence of children but to the artless, ecstatic enthusiasm of children, to dissolve into true nature."

The attempt by Mimei and his coterie to recapture the ethos of a vanishing Japan resonates with the famous ethnographer Yanagita Kunio's (1875–1962) *Tōno monogatari* (Tales of Tōno, 1910), and the founding of folklore studies. Purporting to record the tales of a storyteller from a remote rural area of northern Japan, recent scholarship on *Tales of Tōno* has established how these stories were rewritten by Yanagita to convey to urban, educated Japanese, a portrait of a disappearing constellation of customs and traditions, and to lament the passing of this "world we have lost" in ways that were informed by contemporary ethnographic debates.[9]

The flagship of Taishō era children's literature, *Akai tori*, edited by Suzuki Miekichi, was founded in 1918 to rescue children's literature from what it declared in its inaugural issue were unrefined popular publications that "violate the purity of children." The opening roster of fourteen supporting writers includes some of the most influential literary luminaries of the day, including Tokuda Shūsei, Arishima Ikuo, Akutagawa Ryūnosuke, Kitahara Hakushū, Nogami Toyoichirō, Nogami Yaeko, Shimazaki Tōson, and Izumi Kyōka. Many other prominent literary figures would become regular *Akai tori* contributors in its run of 196 issues, until 1936.

By the late 1920s, the preeminence of children's stories was challenged by those, influenced by Proletarian literature, who wrote juvenilia under the banner of the "children's literature movement" (*jidō bungaku undō*). These works sought to portray realistic circumstances, often emphasizing problem resolution or political and social dimensions of children's lives, denouncing, in the slogan of the day, "feudalist images of children." Rapidly escalating state repression of Proletarian literature in the early 1930s severely curtailed outlets for publication of children's literature that presented unflattering portraits and risked incurring the ire of censors. In the postwar era, the term children's literature (*jidō bungaku*) would be stripped of its association with the Proletarian movement, and applied to an increasingly broad array of styles and perspectives.

The selections by Yukie Ohta in this volume span three decades and encompass a wide spectrum of styles and themes by major authors. The five poems in this collection, all set to music soon after initial publication in the late 1910s or early 1920s, are among the most familiar lullabies in contemporary Japan. Western readers should appreciate the exotic and modern connotations conveyed in these verses: canaries, acacias, white clock towers and blue-eyed dolls invoke imagery far outside the confines of a Japanese village or folk tradition, but as popular expressions of children's culture, they would become emblematic of a new Japan, more liberal, cosmopolitan and progressive.

Journals for children, such as *Akai tori*, had a major role in disseminating youth culture throughout Japan, as well a creating a commonly shared body of literature. For example, Saijō Yaso's

"Canary" first appeared as a poem in November 1918 in *Akai tori*, and six months later reappeared in the same journal set to the music of Narita Tamezō (1893–1945), a famous composer of children's songs. According to one adult male reader in his letter to the editor one year later, he was overjoyed to come upon a group of local children singing "Canary" on Mt. Hakuba, high in the Japanese Alps.

The children's stories here were published over a wider period, from 1920 to the early postwar era. As the reader will observe, the stories sharply contrast with their contemporary children's literature in America: the "family story"—the orthodox genre from 1900–1960—that reassured children of the safety, security and stability available from adults, even as it celebrates the separate world of childhood. These Japanese works both exemplify and challenge the brief tour d'horizon of the history of children's literature—from folktales, to children's stories and juvenilia—offered in this introduction. Each reader should use this sketch of the world in which these works were written to interrogate and engage the writing and, hopefully, to enjoy the often unanticipated perspectives on childhood represented in them.

Notes

1. John Bester's translation of Miyazawa Kenji, *Matasaburo the Wind Imp* (Tokyo: Kodansha International,1992) is no longer in print, and not widely available.

2. Ann Herring's *Edo jidō tosho e no izanai* (An invitation to Edo children's books) (Tokyo: Kumon shuppan, 1988) offers an alternative interpretation.

3. The extensive use of full-page Japanese illustrations in A.B. Mitford's (Lord Redesdale) *Tales of Old Japan* (London: Richard Clay and Sons, 1871), and William Elliot Griffis' *Japanese Fairy World: Stories from the Wonder-Lore of Japan* (Schenectady: James H. Barhyte,1880) underscored, for Western readers, the connection with children. This presumption would be reiterated in a series of postwar children's books by Yoshiko Uchida and Florence Sakade. Cf. Yasuko Makino's *Japan Through Children's Eyes: A Critical Bibliography* (Durham: East Asian Studies Occasional Papers, Number 5, Duke University) 1978.

4. Kan Tadamichi, *Nihon no jidō bungaku* (Japanese children's literature) (Tokyo: Ōtsuki shoten, 1956); Kami Shōichirō, *Nihon jidō bungaku no shisō* (Intellectual origins of Japanese children's literature) (Tokyo: Fūdo sha, 1976)

Torigoe Shin, *Nihon jidō bungaku annai* (An invitation of children's literature) (Tokyo: Riron sha, 1976); Nihon Jidō Bungaku Gakkai, ed. *Nihon jidō bungaku shi o toinaosu,* Vol. 3. (Revisiting the history of Japanese children's literature) (Tokyo: Tokyo shoseki, 1995).

5. Torigoe, *Nihon jidō bungaku annai*, p. 38.

6. Carol Gluck, *Japan's Modern Myths* (Princeton: Princeton University Press, 1987), pp. 186–204.

7. Frederik L. Schodt, *Manga! Manga! The World of Japanese Comics.* (Tokyo: Kodansha International, 1983), p. 51.

8. Two versions of Mimei's essay appeared in 1926, both in the journal *Waseda bungaku* (Waseda literature) and, for a much wider readership, in the *Tokyo nichinichi Shimbun* (Tokyo daily newspaper). Torigoe, *Nihon jidō bungaku annai* pp. 59–60.

9. Marilyn Ivy, *Discourses of the Vanishing: Modernity, Phantasma*, Japan (Chicago: University of Chicago Press, 1995), pp. 66–140.

A Rainbow in the Desert

MATASABURŌ RIDES THE WIND

Miyazawa Kenji

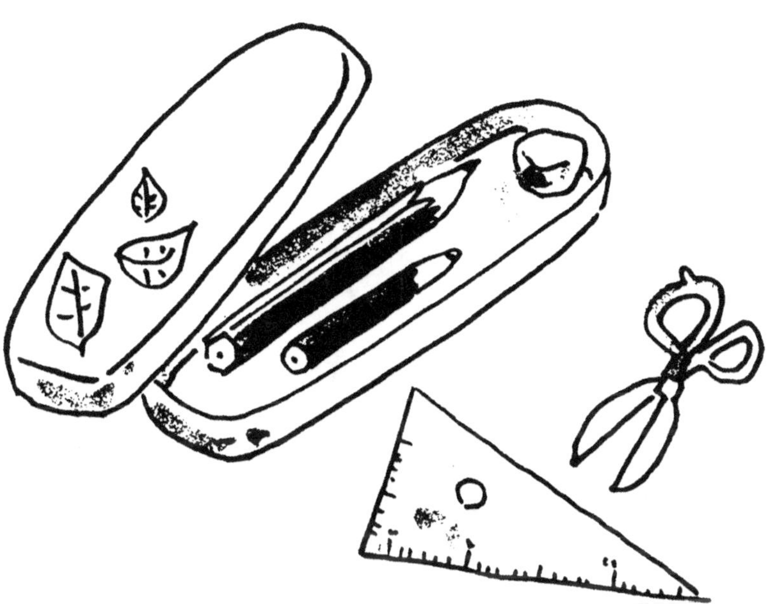

September 1

doh dohdoh dohdohhdoh . . .
Blow away the green walnuts,
and the sour quinces too!
doh dohdoh dohdohhdoh . . .

There was a small school on the bank of a river in a valley. The school had only one classroom, but there were students from the first to the sixth grade. The playground was barely the size of a tennis court, and right behind it was a beautiful hill with chestnut trees. At the corner of the playground flowed an ice-cold waterfall.

It was a fresh September morning. The sky was blue, a strong wind was blowing, and sunlight filled the playground. Two first-graders wearing black pants came up from the river bank. Seeing that no one else had arrived, they cheerfully entered through the gate shouting one after the other, "Hey, we're the first ones! We're first!" But on glancing through the classroom window, they suddenly stiffened with fright, and as they looked at each other, they began to shiver. One of the boys started to cry. In the silent classroom, a completely unfamiliar, odd-looking, red-haired boy sat very properly at the first desk. This desk belonged to the boy outside who was crying. The other boy, who was already half crying himself, was staring wide-eyed into the classroom when someone shouted, "Hey, you! Hey, you!"

Like a giant crow, Kasuke came bounding into the playground with his schoolbag under his arm, immediately followed by Satarō, Kōsuke, and others.

"Why's he crying? What's wrong?" asked Kasuke, grasping the shoulder of the boy who wasn't crying. Just then, that boy began to cry too. Thinking that this was all very strange, the others glanced around and saw the strange red-haired boy sitting in the classroom looking very much at home. Everyone fell silent. The girls also began to gather around, but no one said a word. The red-haired boy, who did not seem the least bit frightened, continued to sit very properly, staring straight at the blackboard.

Then Ichirō arrived. Taking large strides like an adult, he came over to them and asked, "What happened?"

All at once, everyone began speaking and pointing fingers at the strange boy inside the classroom. Ichirō looked toward the classroom for a few seconds. Then, firmly gripping his schoolbag, he went quickly up to the window. Everyone else followed him enthusiastically.

"Who are you? Who's in the classroom before it's time to go

in?" said Ichirō, as he hoisted himself up to the window and stuck his head inside.

"The teacher will scold you for being in the classroom when the weather is so nice!" said Kōsuke from below the window.

"Don't say I didn't warn you!" said Kasuke.

"Get out of there quickly! Get out!" shouted Ichirō. But the red-haired child only glanced around the room and then at the other children, remaining seated in his chair with his hands in his lap.

The boy was very peculiar indeed. He wore a big gray jacket with white shorts and red leather shoes. His face was as red as a ripe apple and his eyes were perfect black circles. It seemed as if he did not understand what everyone was saying. Ichirō was completely puzzled.

"He's a foreigner! And he's going to go to our school!" everyone clamored.

"He's going to be a third-grader!" shouted Kasuke suddenly. The younger children all agreed with him, but Ichirō silently tilted his head skeptically. The strange child glanced over in their direction once or twice and remained seated.

The wind began to blow. The glass doors of the classroom rattled, and the reeds and chestnut trees on the hill behind the school rustled ominously. The boy in the classroom seemed to smirk as he shifted slightly.

"I've got it. He's Matasaburō of the Wind!" Kasuke shouted.

Everyone agreed with Kasuke.

Suddenly, Gorō shouted from the rear, "Ouch! That hurts!" The children turned around to see Gorō angrily punching Kōsuke and accusing him of stepping on his toes. Kōsuke got angry too and punched Gorō back, saying, "Hey! It was your fault. Why are you punching me?"

Gorō, his eyes filled with tears, tried to tackle Kōsuke. At that point, Ichirō got between them and Kasuke stepped in to pull Kōsuke back.

"If you guys fight, the teacher will send you to his office," Ichirō said, glancing toward the classroom.

Ichirō suddenly stopped short. There was no trace of the strange boy who had been sitting in the classroom. Everyone felt sad, as if a beloved pet pony had been given away, or a sparrow they had caught had escaped. The wind blew again, making the windows rattle. The reeds on the hill behind them swayed like pale blue waves.

"It's because you were fighting that Matasaburō disappeared," Kasuke said angrily. The others also thought this was true. Gorō, who was truly sorry that he had started the fight, stood despondently, forgetting all about his injured foot.

"That really was Matasaburō of the Wind," someone said.

"He came because the typhoon season is starting," said someone else.

"He was wearing shoes."

"And he was dressed."

"His hair was red and curly."

"Oh, boy! Matasaburō left a stone on my desk!" said a second-grader, and everyone looked over to see a dirty rock sitting on top of his desk.

"Oh, and he broke that window over there, too."

"No, that's not true. That's where Kaichi threw that stone before vacation."

Just when someone else replied, "No, you're wrong!" the teacher came out holding a shiny whistle in his right hand. As the teacher prepared for assembly, the red-haired boy shuffled out behind him, wearing a white hat and walking proudly, just like a *bodhisattva.*

Everyone fell silent.

"Good morning, teacher!" Ichirō finally said.

"Good morning, teacher!" everyone repeated.

"Good morning everyone. I hope everyone is well. Now then, line up please."

The teacher blew his whistle. The sound reached the mountain on the far side of the valley and then came echoing back. The students lined up with other members of their grades, feeling suddenly as if they had never even been on vacation at all. One sixth-grader, seven fifth-graders, six fourth-graders, and twelve third-graders lined up, in order. Eight second-graders and four first-graders stood in single file at arm's length from one another.

As the students were lining up, the strange child bit the side of his tongue as if something strange or funny were going on. He stood behind the teacher, staring at the rest of the class. The teacher told "Mr. Takada" to come forward. He brought him to the fifth-graders' line, and after comparing his height with Kasuke's, he had him stand between Kasuke and Kiyo, who was behind him. Everyone turned around and stared.

The teacher returned to the doorway and called everyone to attention. The students formed perfectly straight lines at first, but in order to see what the strange boy was doing, they kept turning their heads and looking at him out of the corners of their eyes. Sabarō faced forward properly and confidently stretched out both of his arms so that his fingers were almost touching Kasuke's back, which made Kasuke feel strangely ticklish and uncomfortable.

"At ease!" the teacher said. "Forward march, beginning with the first-graders."

With this command, the first-graders began to walk forward, followed by the second- and third-graders. They circled around in front of everyone else and went through the entranceway to the shoe closet. When the fifth-graders began to walk, the new boy followed Kasuke, strutting like a king. The children in front kept looking back at him, and those who were still waiting to march also stared.

Before long, they had all put their shoes in the closet and entered the classroom. They sat down at their desks in exactly the same order as when they had been lined up outside. The new child sat nonchalantly behind Kasuke.

The whole class was immediately in an uproar.

"Hey, I have a different desk!" someone shouted.

"Hey, there's a piece of rock in my desk!"

"Kiko, Kiko, did you bring your report card? I forgot mine."

"Hey, you! Lend me your pencil! Lend me your pencil!"

"That's not right! You shouldn't take someone else's notebook."

Just then, the teacher came in. Still shouting to one another across the room, the students all stood up and Ichirō gave the command to bow. Only while bowing did the students become silent, and then the uproar began again.

"Quiet, everyone! Quiet!" said the teacher.

"Shh! Etsuji, be quiet. Kasuke, Kiko, hey!" said Ichirō, scolding those who were being the noisiest. Everyone became quiet.

"I hope you all enjoyed your long summer vacation," the teacher said. "I hope you were able to swim all day long and climb in the woods higher than the falcons. I suppose you also tagged along with your older brothers to go thatch gathering in the upper fields. But now vacation is over and the fall semester has begun. They say that autumn is the time when your body and mind are most alert, the best time for learning. Therefore, starting today, let's all study hard together. During this vacation, our circle of friends has increased by one. This is Mr. Takada. His father has come to the upper fields on business. Until recently, Mr. Takada was in a school in Hokkaido, but starting today he will be your classmate, so please study with him at school, and invite him to go chestnut gathering and fishing with you. Do you all understand? Raise your hand if you understand."

All the children's hands went up immediately. The new boy also raised his hand enthusiastically, which made the teacher laugh a little.

"So you understand? Very well then," the teacher said, and the children lowered their hands as quickly as a light going out.

"Teacher!" Kasuke said, raising his hand again.

"Yes?" said the teacher, pointing to Kasuke.

"What is Mr. Takada's first name?"

"It's Saburō."

"Wow! Great! So he is Matasaburō after all."

Kasuke drummed his hands inside his desk. The older children all laughed, but everyone from the third grade down felt a little scared and silently looked at Saburō.

"I hope you all brought your report cards and homework notebooks today. Those of you who brought them, please put them on your desks. I'm coming around to collect them now," the teacher said.

The students noisily opened their bags and put their report cards and homework notebooks on top of their desks. Starting with the first-graders, the teacher began collecting them.

Suddenly, everyone became tense and nervous. A man was standing at the back of the classroom. He wore a baggy white linen suit with a shiny black handkerchief around his neck in place of a necktie, and in his hand he held a white fan. He fanned his face and smiled slightly as he looked down at the students. Everyone gradually became silent and very stiff, but the teacher did not seem particularly bothered. He continued collecting the report cards. Saburō did not have a report card or a homework notebook. He sat with his hands on his desk, and the teacher passed him without saying a word. When he had finished, he walked back to the dais.

"I will correct the homework notebooks and hand them back next Saturday. Those of you who did not bring them today, don't forget them tomorrow. That means Etsuji, Kōji, and Ryōsaku. That's all for today. Starting tomorrow, be prepared every day. The fourth- and sixth-graders will stay after school to clean the classroom today. That's all."

Ichirō gave the order to stand and everyone stood up at once. The man in the back also put down his fan and stood up.

"Bow," Ichirō ordered. The teacher and the students bowed. The man in the back also bowed his head slightly. The younger children rushed out of the classroom, but the fourth-graders lingered behind.

Saburō went up to the man in the baggy white suit. The teacher also stepped down from the dais and approached him.

"Thank you very much for everything," the man said politely, as he bowed to the teacher.

"I am certain he will soon make many friends," said the teacher, returning the bow.

"Please look after my son," he said, politely bowing again.

The man signaled to Saburō with his eyes that he would meet him outside and then and walked through the doorway. Saburō steadied his gaze, feeling the other students staring at him. He then ran outside to catch up with the man. They crossed through the playground and walked upstream along the river. As they left the playground, Saburō glanced back at the school and the students, and then continued walking with the man in the white suit.

"Teacher, is that man his father?" asked Ichirō, holding a broom.

"Yes, he is."

"Why did he come here?"

"At the entrance to the upper fields, there is an ore called molybdenum. He came to mine it."

"Where is it?"

"I'm not quite sure, but I think it's a little down the river from the place where people bring their horses."

"What do you do with molybdenum?"

"You mix it with iron and make medicine with it."

"Does Matasaburō dig too?" asked Kasuke.

"It's not Matasaburō, its Saburō Takada," said Satarō.

"It's Matasaburō! It's Matasaburō!" insisted Kasuke, his face turning completely red.

"Kasuke, if you're going to stay around, why don't you help us clean?" said Ichirō.

"No way! Today's the fourth- and sixth-graders!"

Kasuke dashed out of the classroom and escaped.

The wind began to blow, making the windows rattle. A small black wave formed in the bucket of dirty water and rags.

September 2

The next day Ichirō went early to meet Kasuke, wondering whether or not that strange boy was really going to come to school every day, the way everyone else did. Kasuke was even more curious, and was already waiting for Ichirō when he came. The two boys talked about the new student on the way to school.

By the time they arrived, seven or eight of the younger children had already gathered in the playground and were playing hide the stick, but the new boy had not yet come. Thinking that he might already be in the classroom as he had been the day before, they peeked inside, but no one was there. There was a vague residue of chalk on the blackboard where it had been wiped with a rag during cleaning time the day before.

"He isn't here yet," said Ichirō.

"Uh uh," said Kasuke, looking around.

Ichirō went up to the exercise bar and hoisted himself up. Sliding over to the right, he sat on the edge and waited, gazing in the direction that Saburō had gone the day before. The river glistened and the reeds on the mountain occasionally made white waves indicating that the wind was blowing. Kasuke also waited under the exercise bar.

The two boys did not have to wait long, for all of a sudden, Saburō appeared on the road below, running with his gray school bag under his arm.

"He's coming!" Ichirō inadventently screamed down to Kasuke.

Saburō quickly came up the river bank, and as he approached the gate he said, in a very clear voice, "Good morning!"

Everyone turned around and looked his way, but nobody responded. This was because although everyone had learned to always say good morning to the teacher, they had never said good morning to each other. Saburō's sudden and energetic greeting took Ichirō, Kasuke, and the others by surprise, and made them uneasy. Instead of saying the words "good morning," they ended up mumbling nonsense.

Saburō, not seeming to notice, took two or three steps forward and stood glancing around the playground with his pitch-black eyes. It seemed as if he were searching for someone to play with. Everyone looked curiously over at Saburō, stirring uneasily, and then resumed playing hide the stick. No one went over to him.

Saburō glanced around the playground once more. Then, as if to measure the length of the playground, he began walking with big steps, counting them as he went along. Ichirō quickly jumped off the exercise bar and stood next to Kasuke. They both looked on, holding their breath. Before long, Saburō reached the front of the school. Turning to face everyone, he stood for a while with his head tilted as if he were doing some sort of calculation. Everyone stared over at him curiously. Saburō, looking a little troubled, crossed his arms behind his back, walked past the teacher's office and headed for the river bank.

At that moment, the wind began to blow. The grass along the

river rustled and the dust from the playground was blown into a small tornado shaped like an upside down bottle that rose up higher than the roof.

"I was right. He is Matasaburō of the Wind. Whenever he does anything, the wind always starts to blow," Kasuke said very loudly.

"Yeah," said Ichirō. He was not actually sure if it was really so, but he kept his doubts to himself and just looked over at Saburō, who continued walking quickly toward the river bank.

The teacher came out of the entranceway, holding a whistle as usual.

"Good morning," said the smaller children, flocking around.

"Good morning," said the teacher. He glanced around the playground, blew his whistle, and told everyone to line up.

The students gathered together and lined up in order, just as they had done the previous day. Saburō, too, stood just where he had been told the day before. Because the sun was shining so brightly, the teacher squinted a little as he told everyone to go inside, and one by one they entered the classroom.

After everyone had bowed, the teacher said, "We will begin our studies today. I hope you all brought your supplies. First- and second-graders take out your calligraphy models and ink stones; third- and fourth-graders take out your arithmetic texts, notebooks, and pencils; and fifth- and sixth-graders, please take out your Japanese books."

The students began shuffling their belongings around. During the commotion, Satarō, who sat at the desk right next to Saburō's, suddenly reached across and grabbed a pencil from Kayo, a third-grader. Kayo was Satarō's younger sister.

"Don't take my pencil!" Kayo screamed, and tried to get it back.

"It's mine," Satarō said, as he put it in his breast pocket and shoved his hands into his sleeves like a Chinaman does when he bows. He pressed his chest tightly against his desk.

"You lost your pencil in the shed the day before yesterday. Give it back! Give it back!" Kayo said, standing up as she struggled to get the pencil. Satarō was stuck to his desk like a petrified crab. Kayo, still standing, opened her mouth very wide as if she were about to cry. Seeing this, Saburō placed his Japanese book on his desk with a troubled look on his face. And when he saw tears begin to pour out of Kayo's eyes, Saburō took the stubby pencil that he was holding in his right hand and placed it in front of Satarō without saying a word. Satarō suddenly sprang to life and sat up abruptly.

"You're giving it to me?" he asked Saburō, who seemed a little embarrassed.

"Yes," Saburō said with resignation.

Satarō laughed out loud. He took the pencil out of his breast pocket and placed it in Kayo's little pink hand.

Meanwhile, the teacher was helping the first-graders to mix their ink and did not see what Saburō had done. Because Kasuke sat in front of Saburō, he did not notice either. Ichirō was the only one who saw what happened. What he saw gave him a strange feeling and left him speechless. He sat quietly in his seat with his teeth clenched.

"Before we take our break, the third-graders must do some more subtraction problems. Please try this one," the teacher said, writing "25 minus 12" on the blackboard. The third-graders all eagerly copied this into their notebooks. Kayo had her face nearly pressed against her book as she wrote.

"Fourth-graders, do this problem," he said and wrote "17 times 14." The fourth-graders, Satarō, Yoshizō, Kōsuke, and the others, all copied it down.

"Fifth-graders, open your readers to lesson 3 on page 10 and read as much as you can, writing down any words you do not know in your workbooks."

The fifth-graders began to do as they were told.

"Ichirō, you open your reader to page 18 and also write down any words you do not know."

The teacher stepped down from the dais and walked around, looking over the first- and second-graders' calligraphy.

Saburō held his book on his desk with both hands and read the passage, seemingly without breathing, and without copying any words into his notebook. Whether it was because there really were no words he did not know or because he had given his only pencil to Satarō, nobody knew.

Before long, the teacher returned to the dais. He wrote the answers to the third- and fourth-graders' arithmetic problems and put up new ones. Then he wrote the words that the fifth-graders did not know on the blackboard and also wrote their pronunciation and the meaning.

"Kasuke, please read aloud," he said, and Kasuke read from his book, getting stuck two or three times. Saburō listened silently. After Kasuke had read only ten lines, the teacher told him to stop and began reading the next section himself. When everyone had read, he instructed them to put away their supplies.

"That's all for now," he said, and stood on the dais.

Ichirō called the class to attention. After the students bowed, they all went outside, in order, and without lining up this time, they broke up into groups and played.

During second period, the teacher came out with his mandolin. They all sang songs, and Saburō knew all the songs too. This period passed very quickly.

During third period, the third- and fourth-graders studied Japanese, and the fifth- and sixth-graders studied arithmetic. The teacher wrote problems on the blackboard and had the students solve them.

After a little while, Ichirō wrote the answers on the blackboard. As he was writing, he glanced over in Saburō's direction and saw him scratching his calculations into his notebook with a small piece of charcoal. Where he got the charcoal was a mystery.

Sunday, September 4

On Sunday morning, the sky was very clear and the river sparkled. Ichirō met Kasuke, Satarō, and Etsuji, and together they walked toward Saburō's house, crossing the river a little downstream from the school. They had each broken off a branch from a willow tree and peeled its blue-green bark to make a switch. Swinging their sticks, they climbed the path that led to the upper fields. They climbed so quickly that they got out of breath.

"I wonder if Matasaburō is really waiting for us at the spring," one of them said.

"He's waiting. He wouldn't lie."

"Oh, its so hot. It would be nice if the wind would blow."

"The wind is blowing from somewhere."

"Matasaburō made it blow."

"The sun looks kind of hazy."

There were some small white clouds forming in the sky. The boys had already climbed a long way, and they could see all the houses in the valley below. The roof of Ichirō's barn glared white in the sunlight.

The path turned into the woods, and for a while they could not see around them. The ground was damp. They soon arrived at the spring where they had arranged to meet. They heard Saburō's voice call out, "Hey, did you all make it?"

The boys climbed quickly. Saburō stood at the bend of the path. His little lips were pressed firmly shut as he watched the three of them coming toward him. They finally got to the spot where Saburō was standing, but they were panting so hard that at first they did not say anything.

Kasuke gasped as he tried to take a deep breath.

"I've been waiting for a long time. I heard it's going to rain today," said Saburō.

"Then we should hurry. But first let's have a drink."

The boys wiped the sweat off their flushed faces and drank many handfuls of the cold water that poured over a white rock in the spring.

"My house is close by. It's just above that valley over there. Let's stop there on the way back," Saburō suggested.

"Okay, but let's go to the field first."

As they started on their way, the spring gurgled and the trees seemed to rustle, as if to tell them something. The boys trudged through the thicket at the edge of the woods and passed over rough terrain. Rocks crumbled under their feet as they headed west. Beyond the sunny hills and shady hills that overlapped into the distance, they could see green fields spreading out along the river.

"Hey, look at the river!" one of the boys exclaimed.

"It looks like the sash of the Kasuga god," said Saburō.

"Like what?" asked Ichirō.

"The sash of the Kasuga god."

"Have you really seen a god's sash?"

"I saw it in Hokkaido."

None of the others knew what he was talking about and they all fell silent.

At last, they arrived at the entrance to the upper fields. On the freshly cut grass stood a huge chestnut tree with a big black hole burned into its trunk. Straw ropes and broken sandals were suspended from its branches.

"If we go a little farther we'll see lots of people cutting the grass to make thatch. There's also a place with horses," said Ichirō, as he started walking along a path in the grass.

Saburō started walking next. "There aren't any bears here, so I guess its okay to let the horses run around," he said.

After a while they came to a big oak tree. Under the tree was a large bag made out of straw rope that someone had left behind. Many bales of grass were scattered around. Two horses with bundles on their backs snorted when they saw Ichirō.

"Big brother. Are you there? Big brother, we're here!" called out Ichirō, wiping the sweat off of his face.

"Hey, stay where you are. I'm coming." From a far-away hollow they heard the voice of Ichirō's older brother. The sun suddenly brightened as he emerged from the tall grass, smiling.

"Welcome! I see you brought everyone. Welcome. When you go back, you'll have to take the horses with you. It's going to get cloudy this afternoon. After I gather some more grass, I'll be finished here. You guys stay by the river bank and play. There are still twenty horses in the pasture." As he started to leave, he turned back and said, "Don't leave the river bank. It could be dangerous if you get lost. I'll be back at noon."

"Okay, we'll be down by the river bank," Ichirō said.

Ichirō's brother went back to work. Thin clouds floated in the sky and the sun glistened like a mirror. A gust of wind made the uncut grass rustle.

Ichirō started walking first, following a small path that soon led to the river bank. A fence made of logs kept the horses from straying out of the pasture. Etsuji tried to creep under the logs, but Kasuke stopped him. "Let's take one off," he said, and pulled down the end of one of the logs so that everyone could get to the other side. A little way off, where the grass was tall, seven horses with shiny coats had gathered and were gently swinging their tails.

"These horses are probably worth over a thousand yen each. Starting next year they're going to be in the horse races," Ichirō said, going up to them.

The horses came toward him as if they were enjoying the attention and stretched their muzzles out to signal that they wanted something.

"They want salt," everyone said in unison. They stretched out their hands to let the horses lick them. Saburō stood back with his hands in his pockets. He was not used to being around horses.

"Hey, you're afraid of horses!" said Etsuji.

"Who me? I'm not afraid!" Saburō responded, and took his hand out of his pocket, stretching it toward one of the horses. The horse extended its neck and stuck its tongue out. Saburō turned pale and quickly stuck his hand back in his pocket.

"You're afraid of horses!" Etsuji said again. Saburō turned completely red and stood for a moment uneasily, but then said, "Let's have a horse race."

The others wondered what exactly he meant by a horse race.

"I've been to the horse races lots of times," Saburō continued, "but none of these horses have saddles so we can't ride them. How about if everyone chases a horse and whichever one reaches that big tree over there is the winner?"

"This guy's crazy," said Kasuke. "The herdsman is going to get you."

"It's okay. Racehorses need to practice," Saburō insisted.

"Okay, then, this horse is mine," said one of the boys, choosing a horse.

"This one's mine."

"All right, then, this one's mine."

Everyone took a willow branch or a reed and lightly whipped the horses, but the horses didn't even flinch. Instead, they lowered their heads to eat some grass, then raised their heads as if to take a long look at the scenery. Finally, Ichirō clapped his hands together and said, "Go!" All of a sudden the horses began running.

"Wow!" Kasuke shouted, as he jumped up and ran after his horse. But somehow it was not the same thing as a horse race. The horses did not run as fast as they would have in a real horse race. Still, everyone was having a great time chasing after them.

The horses ran a little way, and then seemed as if they were going to stop short. The boys were panting and gasping a little, but they kept running after the horses. Before they realized it, the horses had turned around, and started back toward the place where the four boys had entered the pasture.

"The horses are running away! They're running away! Stop them! Stop them!" Ichirō shouted, turning blue in the face. It looked as if the horses were going to get away. They headed for the log fence. Ichirō ran as fast as he could crying, "Whoa! Whoa! Whoa!" When he reached the fence, Ichirō looked as if he were about to fall over. He waved his arms above his head, but two horses had already gotten out.

"Come quick and catch them! Come quick!" Ichirō shouted, nearly out of breath, as he put back the log. The three boys scurried under the logs to find the two escaped horses standing right outside the pasture, pulling up grass with their teeth.

"Sneak up on them slowly. Slowly," Ichirō said, firmly grasping one horse by the bit in its mouth. As Kasuke and Saburō approached the other horse, it became frightened and began running at full speed along the river bank.

"Big brother, a horse is escaping! A horse is escaping! Big brother, a horse is escaping!" Ichirō yelled at the top of his lungs, as Saburō and Kasuke ran after the horse with all their might. This time it really seemed as if the horse wanted to escape. It ran through uncut grass that was almost as high as the top of its head, and then through shorter grass.

Kasuke's legs grew numb and he soon became disoriented. Everything around him turned pale and started spinning around until at last he fell down in the tall grass. As he was falling, he caught a glimpse of the horse's red mane and the white hat on Saburō's head following close behind.

Kasuke lay flat on his back and looked up at the sky. The sky was stark white and spun in circles overhead. Thin gray clouds moved rapidly and Kasuke's heart was beating quickly. When he finally got up, his breathing was uneven. He started walking in the direction that the horse had gone. There was a faint path of bent grass that seemed to have been made by the horse and Saburō when they had passed by. Kasuke chuckled and then thought to himself, "Hm. The horse is probably scared, just standing around somewhere."

He continued along the trail, but before he had gone a hundred steps, in the midst of beautiful, high thistle, the trail mysteriously split into two or three paths and he couldn't figure out which one to take.

"Hey!" Kasuke yelled. He thought he heard Saburō calling back, "Hey!" somewhere off in the distance.

He made up his mind to follow the middle path. Along the way, the path broke off in places and cut across steep slopes where there didn't seem to be any footprints.

The sky became very dark and heavy. Everything grew dim and a cold wind passed over the grass. Wisps of clouds and fog floated in front of his eyes.

"Oh, this is terrible. And it's going to get worse," thought Kasuke. Just at that moment, the horse's tracks disappeared from the grass completely.

"Oh, it's getting worse, it's getting worse," Kasuke thought, his heart pounding.

The grass swayed in the wind. The fog thickened and Kasuke's clothes were damp all the way through. Kasuke called out at the top of his lungs, "Ichirō, Ichirō, over here!" but he heard no reply. Like the chalk powder that comes off a blackboard, a cold dark cloud of mist danced around him and everything became silent and gloomy. He could hear droplets of mist settling on the grass. Kasuke wanted to find Ichirō and the others, so he turned back. Strangely, everything looked different from the way it had been before. The thistle had grown thicker, and stones seemed to have rolled onto the grass where there had been no stones before.

Suddenly, the biggest valley he had ever seen appeared before his eyes. The pampas grass rustled and, like the bottom of the valley, seemed to disappear in the fog. When the wind blew, the pampas grass waved its many thin arms in all directions as if to say, "Oh, hello, west. Hello, east, west, south. Hello, west." Kasuke closed his eyes and quickly turned back. He noticed a small black path in the grass made by many horses' hoofs. Kasuke laughed lightly and walked steadily along the path, almost in a trance. The path kept getting wider and then narrower again, and it seemed to be going in circles. Kasuke came upon a big chestnut tree that was burned at the top, where the path once again split in several directions. This was probably the place where all the horses gathered. It appeared to Kasuke, through the fog, to be a round clearing.

Kasuke was disheartened. He turned around and started back in the direction he had come from. A type of flower that he did not recognize silently quivered as he passed. A strong wind blew through the grass as if it were warning him of an impending doom. The sky became crystal clear, and then right before his eyes appeared something that looked like a big black house. For a while, Kasuke could not believe his eyes and remained standing where he was. Finally convinced that it was a house, he approached it timidly and looked, only to find that it was just a big black rock. The sky spun around and around and the grass shook off droplets of water.

"If we get lost and end up on the other side of the plain, Matasaburō and I will die for sure," he muttered half out loud, half to himself. Then he cried out, "Ichirō, Ichirō! Are you there, Ichirō?"

The sky became bright again and the grass breathed in delight.

"The son of the electrician from Isado village got tied up by a mountain man." Those words, which someone had once spoken to him, now came to him.

Suddenly the trail disappeared. For some time, there was not a sound. Then a strong wind began to blow. The sky sparkled and rippled like a waving flag. Sparks flew from the heavens. Kasuke lay down and fell fast asleep in the grass. He felt as if everything that had happened were something out of a fairy tale.

Saburō stood over Kasuke with his feet spread apart, looking up at the sky. He wore a shiny overcoat made of glass over his usual gray jacket, and glass shoes. The blue shadow of a chestnut tree fell on Saburō's shoulders and Saburō's blue shadow fell on the grass. The wind was blowing and blowing. Saburō did not smile or speak. He only looked up at the sky with his mouth closed tightly. Suddenly, he lept up into the sky. His glass coat sparkled.

By chance, Kasuke opened his eyes at that moment. The gray fog parted to reveal the horse standing peacefully in front of him. It looked as if it were afraid of Kasuke and averted its eyes. Kasuke jumped up and caught the horse by its name tag. Saburō came up behind him, his almost colorless lips shut tightly. Kasuke trembled.

"Hey!" The voice of Ichirō's brother could be heard through the fog. They also heard thunder.

"Hey, Kasuke! Are you there?" Ichirō's voice said.

Elated, Kasuke jumped up and shouted, "Hey! I'm over here! I'm over here!"

Before he knew it, Ichirō and his brother were standing before him, and Kasuke began to cry.

"We've been looking for you. We were so worried. Look at you! You're all wet!" said Ichirō's brother. His trained hands held the horse's neck and quickly slipped a bit over the horse's mouth.

"Okay, let's go," he said.

"You scared us, Matasaburō," Ichirō said to Saburō. Saburō remained silent with his lips firmly shut and nodded.

Everyone followed Ichirō's brother down two small hills and along a wide black path. Lightning flashed twice, making the sky turn white. The smell of smoke from burning grass flowed through the fog.

"Grandpa, I found them! I found them all!" yelled Ichirō's brother.

An old man stood in the fog and said to them, "I was worried, so worried. Now I'm so relieved. Kasuke, you must be cold. Come on inside." He treated Kasuke just as if he were his own grandson.

There was a little thatched enclosure at the foot of the chestnut tree with a fire burning inside. Ichirō's brother tied the horse to an oak tree and the horse grunted.

"Oh, you poor boy! You've been crying," said the grandfather. He then turned to Saburō and said, "You're the son of the man who's digging at Kanayama, aren't you? Everyone eat. Eat! I'll fry up some more of these dumplings. How far did you go?"

"To Sasanagane," Ichirō's brother answered.

"That's very dangerous. Very dangerous. Had you gone down into the valley, you and the horse would never have made it back. Hey, Kasuke, eat. You too, Saburō."

"Grandpa, I'll take the horse back," Ichirō's brother said.

"Yes, if the herdsman comes, he'll get angry. But why don't you wait a little while. It'll clear up again right away," the grandfather said. "I was so worried! I even went down to the bottom of the mountain to look for you. I'm so relieved. The rain will let up soon."

"The weather was so good this morning." Ichirō's brother said.

"Yes, and it will get better again. Oh no! The roof is leaking. The rain is getting in," said the grandfather.

Ichirō's brother went outside to fix it. They heard the ceiling rattle and the old man smiled and looked up. Then Ichirō's brother came back in again.

"Grandpa, it's light out again. The rain has stopped," he said.

"Oh, really? Now everyone, warm yourselves well by the fire. I'm going out again to cut grass."

The fog lifted quickly and sunlight came streaming in. The sun leaned a little to the west as all of the leaves and stalks and flowers sucked in the last remaining sunlight of the year. The green fields to the west stopped crying and laughed gaily, and the chestnut tree emitted a blue halo.

They were all tired as they followed Ichirō down from the upper fields. When they reached the spring, Saburō parted from them and headed toward his house alone, without saying a word.

"He is a spirit of the wind after all!" said Kasuke, on the way back home.

"You're wrong!" Ichirō said loudly.

September 5

The next day it rained in the morning, but from second period the sky gradually got brighter, and by the ten-minute break at the end of third period, the rain had stopped completely and patches of blue sky could be seen here and there. Fluffy white clouds ran toward the east as the remaining fog rose like steam from the mountain grasses and the chestnut trees.

"When school's over, let's go pick grapes," Kōsuke whispered to Kasuke.

"Yeah, let's go. Why don't you come too, Matasaburō?" Kasuke said, inviting him.

"Hey, I don't want to show my secret picking spot to Matasaburō!" Kōsuke said, but Saburō, not hearing this, said, "Okay, I'll go. I've gone grape picking in Hokkaido too. My mother used to preserve them in two barrels."

"Can I come too?" asked Shokichi, a second-grader.

"No! I don't want to show it to everybody! I found a new spot," Kōsuke said.

The students could not wait for school to end. When fifth period ended, Ichirō, Kasuke, Satarō, Kōsuke, Etsuji, and Saburō started off upstream. After they had gone a little way, they came to a house with a thatched roof and a small tobacco field in front of it. The lower leaves of the tobacco plants had already been picked and were lined up in piles that resembled a beautiful forest.

"What are these?" said Saburō, as he plucked one of the leaves and showed it to Ichirō. Ichirō was startled and said, turning a little pale, "Hey, Matasaburō. If you steal a tobacco leaf, the Tobacco Man will get you for sure. Matasaburō, why did you take it?"

"The Tobacco Man counts each one of these leaves and writes it down in a notebook. If he catches you, don't blame me!" said one of the boys.

"Me neither!"

"Me neither!" everyone said in unison.

Saburō's face turned bright red and for a while he swung the leaf around trying to think of something to say.

"I didn't know," he said angrily.

All the boys looked fearfully toward the house to see if anyone was watching. Beyond the thick rising steam of the tobacco field, the house was silent. It didn't seem as if anyone was there.

"That's Shōsuke's house. You know—the first-grader." Kasuke said, trying to ease the tension.

From the beginning, Kōsuke had not wanted Saburō and the others to see the new grape vines he had discovered. Now he said, maliciously, "Matasaburō didn't know! He's so dumb!"

Saburō seemed troubled and again was silent for a while, but then said, "If that's the way it is, I'm leaving the leaf here," and gently put the leaf at the foot of the tree where he found it.

"Let's go quickly," Ichirō said, and started walking first. Everyone else followed except for Kōsuke, who remained behind saying to himself, "Matasaburō left that leaf. He left it over there," but everyone kept walking, and finally Kōsuke caught up with the others.

The boys climbed along a narrow trail in the reeds toward the mountain and came to a clearing where chestnut trees and big grape vines grew.

"I found this spot, so everyone don't take too much," Kōsuke said.

"I'm going to pick chestnuts," said Saburō, and picked up a rock and threw it at a branch. A green burr fell to the ground. Saburō opened it with a stick and took out two chestnuts that were still white. Everyone else was busy picking grapes.

As Kōsuke passed under a chestnut tree in search of more grapes, water came pouring down on him. A surprised Kōsuke looked up to see Saburō, sitting in the tree chuckling and wiping his face with his sleeves.

"Hey, Matasaburō, what are you doing?" Kōsuke asked, looking up at him angrily.

"It was the wind," Saburō said laughing.

Kōsuke left the foot of the tree and began picking grapes at another bush. He picked so many grapes that he could barely hold them all, and his mouth turned big and purple like a clown's from eating them.

"Isn't this enough to take back with us?" Ichirō asked.

"I'm going to pick more," Kōsuke said.

Just then, Kōsuke was covered once again with cold water. He looked up startled. This time Saburō was not in the tree, but he saw Saburō's gray elbow sticking out from behind the trunk and heard him laughing. This made Kōsuke extremely angry.

"Hey, Matasaburō. You poured water on me again!"

"It was the wind!" Saburō replied.

Everyone burst out laughing.

"Matasaburō, you shook the tree from over there!" Kōsuke shouted.

Everyone burst out laughing again. Kōsuke said nothing for a while and then looked Saburō in the eye and said, "Matasaburō, the world could do without you."

Matasaburō laughed sheepishly.

"Sorry, Kōsuke," was all he said.

Kōsuke wanted to say something more but was so angry that he could not think of anything to say. He repeated the same thing again. "Hey, Matasaburō. You are the wind, and the world could do without a wind like you."

"I said I was sorry. I did it because you're always so mean to me," Saburō said innocently, blinking his eyes. But this did not melt Kōsuke's anger.

"Hey, Matasaburō, the world could do without you!" he repeated for the third time.

Saburō seemed slightly amused by this and started chuckling. "Tell me why the wind doesn't belong in this world," he said, and pointed his finger at Kōsuke like a teacher does. Kōsuke felt as if he were being tested, and could not do anything but think for a while.

"Because you're mischievous. Because you break umbrellas," Kōsuke said finally.

"And why else?" Saburō prodded, as he took a step forward.

"Because you break trees and blow them over!"

"And why else? Why else?"

"You wreck houses."

"Why else?"

"Because you blow out fires."

"And why else?"

"You blow people's hats off."

"And?"

"And, um, you knock over power lines."

"And? And? And?"

"And you blow roofs off houses."

"Aha, aha! the roof is what shelters the house. Is there anything else? Well? Well?"

"You also blow out lamps."

"Aha, aha! The lamp is what contains the light. But is that all?"

Kōsuke was stumped. He had just given about every reason he could think of. No matter how much he thought, nothing more came to him. Saburō, who was amused, pointed his finger at him once again and said, "Yes? Well? And what else? Huh?"

Kōsuke turned red in the face from thinking so hard, and then finally replied, "You break pinwheels."

Saburō jumped up and laughed. Everyone else also laughed. Together they laughed and laughed and laughed. When Saburō finally stopped laughing, he said, "You finally said pinwheel! If you're a pinwheel, then you don't think that the wind is bad. Of course there are times when the wind breaks them, but most of the time the wind makes them spin. Pinwheels *like* the wind. You are wrong. I was waiting for you to say pinwheel!" Saburō started laughing again until it seemed as if he were going to cry. Kōsuke, who had been really angry, gradually began to forget, and finally started laughing with Saburō, and this put everyone back in a good mood.

"Kōsuke, I'm sorry I was mean to you," Saburō said.

"We should be going now," Ichirō said, handing him five bunches of grapes. Saburō in turn divided up his white chestnuts, giving two to each of the others. They all headed down the path that led back toward their homes.

September 7

The morning was very misty and the mountain behind the school could barely be seen. But as on the day before, the sky gradually cleared and after second period the sun came out. By noon it was as hot as a midsummer day. The younger students looked as if they were about to melt.

In the afternoon, it got so hot that the teacher wiped perspiration off his face as he stood on the dais. While the fourth-graders practiced their calligraphy and the fifth- and sixth-graders drew their drawings, it grew so humid that they started to get drowsy. When classes ended, everyone got together and went down to the river.

"Matasaburō, why don't you come swimming with us? We're going down to join the others," Kasuke asked, inviting Saburō.

They walked downstream, past the trail they had followed to get to the upper fields a few days before. Part of the river split off to the right, forming a wide beach, and just downstream a big honey locust tree grew on the side of a low cliff.

"Hello!" cried the children who had already arrived, raising both arms above their heads.

The boys all darted toward the water through the silk trees as if they were running in a race. They threw off their clothes and dove straight in, splashing with their feet as they swam diagonally across to the far shore. The other children, who were already in the water, swam after them. Saburō took off his clothes and began swimming too. When he got about halfway across, he started laughing out loud.

Ichirō, who had already reached the other side, waited on the river bank with his hair slicked back and his lips purple from the cold water. He stood shivering and asked, "What are you laughing at, Matasaburō?"

Saburō, who was also shivering, stuck his head out of the water and said, "This river is really cold!"

"But why are you laughing, Matasaburō?" asked Ichirō, again.

"The way you guys swim is funny. Why do you splash with your feet like that?" he asked, laughing.

"Hey!" Ichirō exclaimed, feeling a little self-conscious. "Let's play get the rock." He picked up a round white rock.

"Yeah!" shouted the other children.

"I'll drop it from up in that tree, okay?" said Ichirō, as he nimbly climbed up the honey locust tree. "Okay, I'm going to drop it. One, two, three."

He dropped the rock into the swimming hole. The children scrambled with one another and did back flips off the bank into the water to get to the rock, but they all ran out of air before reaching the bottom. They surfaced one by one, spraying water out of their mouths.

Saburō watched very carefully what the others were doing. After everyone had surfaced, he dove under the water—but he, too, ran out of breath before he could reach the bottom. Everyone laughed.

Just then, on the far bank near the silk trees, four men carrying nets came toward them. From the top of the tree, Ichirō whispered to everyone, "Hey, they're going to set off an explosion in the water. Pretend you don't know. Everyone stop playing and go downstream."

The boys casually swam downstream, doing their best not to look toward the grownups. From up in the tree, Ichirō shaded his eyes with his hand to see what was going on downstream, and then dove head-first into the swimming hole and swam under water, catching up with the others. They all stood at the place where the current became strong again.

"Keep playing, like you don't know what's happening," Ichirō said, and all the children went back to collecting stones and such, pretending they did not know anything about the blast that was about to come.

At the far embankment, Shosuke, who worked at the mine, looked around him and then sat cross-legged on the gravel. He slowly took out a tobacco box and held a pipe in his mouth. As he sucked on the pipe, smoke came out the corners of his mouth. Then he took another object out of his pocket.

"It's the bomb! It's the bomb!" The children shouted. Ichirō waved his arms to stop them. Shosuke put the light of his pipe near the object he had taken from his pocket. A man who was standing behind him jumped into the water and set up a net. Shosuke stood up very carefully, put one foot in the water, and threw the object he was holding into the river, below the honey

locust tree. A loud noise was heard, and all the grownups got into the water.

"Okay, they're going to come downstream. Everyone get ready," Ichirō said.

Kōsuke grabbed a small brown singing frog about the size of his little finger that came floating downstream on its side. From behind him, Kasuke made a slurping sound like he was sipping a melon, because he had caught a six-inch-long carp. Everyone had fun catching the fish.

"Be quiet. Be quiet," Ichirō said.

Five or six men, some bare-chested, some wearing T-shirts, came running from the opposite bank. From behind them, a man in a mesh shirt came riding up bare-backed on a horse. It looked like a scene from the movies. Everyone had heard the sound of the blast and came to see what was going on.

Shosuke stood with his arms crossed, watching the others catch fish, but he himself did not catch even one.

"There aren't any," he said.

Saburō threw some fish onto the river bank near Shosuke and said, "Here, I'm returning these to you."

"Who does this guy think he is? He's making fun of me," he said, and glared at Saburō. Saburō said nothing and walked away. Shosuke watched him with a sour face, and everyone burst out laughing.

Shosuke silently walked away upstream and the other men followed after him. The man in the mesh shirt rode away on his horse. Kōsuke swam out and brought back the fish that Saburō had put down. Everyone laughed again.

"That was great! When they set off the blast, all those little fish scattered everywhere!" shouted Kasuke, jumping up and down on the sand.

The children piled up rocks to make a little preserve for the fish they had caught. Even if the fish revived, they would not be able to swim away.

They climbed the honey locust tree in the sweltering heat. Even the silk trees looked utterly exhausted, and the sky seemed to have no limit.

"Hey, he's going to ruin our fish preserve!" someone yelled. They all looked around and saw a man with a strange, sharp nose. He was fully clothed and wore straw sandals, and in his hand he held what appeared to be a cane that he was using to stir the water in the fish pool.

"Hey, he's the Tobacco Man," said Satarō.

"Matasaburō, he found out that you took that tobacco leaf. He's come to get you," Kasuke said.

"Oh yeah? I'm not scared," Saburō said, biting his lip.

"Hey, everyone. Let's hide Matasaburō. Everybody gather around him," Ichirō said.

They placed Saburō on the farthest interior branch of the honey locust tree and sat on the surrounding branches.

The man started walking toward them along the bank.

"He's coming! He's coming!" everyone whispered, holding their breath. But the man did not seem particularly interested in finding Saburō, and passed in front of them.

Just downstream from the swimming hole, where the water was

shallow, the man crossed the river back and forth several times with his dirty sandals and socks on, as if he were trying to wash them. Everyone gradually felt less scared of him, and began to feel bothered by his presence.

"I'm going to say something, so everyone repeat after me on a count of three, okay?" Ichirō said. "The teacher always says, 'Don't muddy the water!' One, two, three."

"The teacher always says, 'Don't muddy the water!' " they all repeated.

The man was startled and looked toward them, but seemed to be unsure whether they had actually said anything. They repeated the chant.

"The teacher always says, 'Don't muddy the water!' "

The man with the sharp nose looked up at them. His mouth was puckered as if he were smoking a cigarette. "Can you drink the water around here?" he asked.

"The teacher always says, 'Don't muddy the water!' "

The man asked, looking a little confused, "Is it forbidden to walk in the river?"

"The teacher always says, 'Don't muddy the water!' " they repeated.

This clearly disturbed the man, but he tried to hide his confusion by deliberately crossing the river very slowly and then diagonally climbing the bank of blue clay and red gravel very carefully. He then disappeared into the tobacco field that was above the river bank.

"He didn't come to get me after all," Saburō said, as he dove into the swimming hole.

Everyone felt a little bit sorry for having teased Saburō and the man with the pointed nose. They jumped off the tree and started swimming back across the river. When they got to the other side, some of the boys wrapped their fish in towels, while others just held them in their hands. They all went home.

September 8

The next morning before school started, the students who had arrived early hung from the parallel bars or played hide the stick. Satarō arrived a little late, carefully carrying a bamboo basket.

"What is it? What is it?" everyone immediately asked, running up to him and looking inside. Satarō tried to cover the basket with the sleeve of his shirt and rushed back to a cave that was behind the school. Everyone followed after him. When Ichirō looked inside, his face turned blue. The basket contained *sanshō* powder, a poison that was illegal, like explosives. People caught using it were taken away by the police.

Satarō hid the basket beside the cave and then casually wandered back into the playground. Everyone whispered to each other about what they had seen until it was time to go inside.

On that day, just as it had done the day before, the temperature began to rise around ten o'clock. The students waited impatiently for class to end. At two o'clock, when fifth period ended, everyone rushed outside. Satarō picked up the bamboo basket from the cave where he had placed it before school. Hiding it with his sleeve, he went down to the river surrounded by his classmates. Saburō followed, along with Kasuke.

They gagged from the smell of the powder, as they did when they smelled the gas lanterns used at the town festivals. When they came to the point on the river where the honey locust tree stood, they ran to their usual swimming hole. The peaks of the beautiful summer clouds rose high in the sky and the honey locust tree sparkled green.

They all hurriedly took off their clothes and stood at the edge of the swimming hole. Satarō said to Ichirō, "Line up and when the fish come floating by, swim out and get them."

The younger children, getting very excited, pushed each other as they stood around the swimming hole. Pekichi and three or four others were already swimming underneath the honey locust tree.

Satarō walked proudly upstream and dunked his basket in the water. Everyone stood silently staring at the water. Saburō did not look at the water. Instead, he watched a black bird flying above a cloud. Ichirō also sat on the bank, slapping a rock with his hand. No matter how long the boys waited, the fish did not come.

Satarō stood watching the water with a very stern look on his face. Everyone thought that if it had been like the day before, when they had set off the explosion, they would have caught as many as ten fish by now. They waited in silence, but not one fish came floating downstream.

"No fish are coming!" Kōsuke called out. This startled Satarō, but he continued to gaze into the water.

"No fish are coming!" Pekichi repeated, from beneath the tree, and then all the boys began repeating the phrase, as they dove into the water.

Satarō stared into the water for a few moments more and then stood up and said, "Why don't we play tag?"

"Yeah, let's play!" they yelled, and stuck their hands out of the water to choose who was to be "it." The ones who were swimming quickly came ashore and also stuck out their hands. Ichirō decided that the slimy clay deposit below the cliff, where the man with the strange pointed nose had walked the day before, was to be the base. That meant that if you stood there, the person who was "it" could not get you.

Etsuji, whose lips had turned deep purple from the cold water, was chosen to be "it" first. He ran into the river and caught Kisaku, and then two people were "it." They all ran around on the river bank and swam in the hole, catching and being caught by one another.

In the end, Saburō alone was "it." Everyone stood beneath the honey locust tree and watched as he caught Kichirō.

"Yoshirō, I'm going to get you too," said Saburō, as Yoshirō stood silently staring at him. Yoshirō then came running downstream, and the others prepared to dive into the hole. But Yoshirō slipped and fell because he had clay on his feet, and everyone shouted and jumped over Yoshirō, plunging into the water to get upstream to the blue clay.

"Come on, Matasaburō," said Kasuke, teasing Saburō by opening his mouth wide and spread his arms.

A frustrated Saburō said, "Okay, watch this," and dove into the water, swimming with all his might toward Kasuke. Saburō's red hair was dripping wet and his lips had turned a little purple, which made him look scary.

The base was small and not everyone could stand on it at once.

It was also on a steep incline, which made it extra slippery. The four or five boys who were at the bottom held onto those above them, trying not to slip and fall into the water. Ichirō sat calmly at the top trying to discuss strategy, and the others all put their heads together and listened.

Saburō swam up and splashed everyone with water, using both hands. When they tried to splash him back, the clay gave way a little and everyone started to slide down a bit. Pleased by this, Saburō splashed them some more. The boys fell into the water all at once, and Saburō tagged them all. He even caught Ichirō. Kasuke was the only one who climbed up over the top and swam away. Saburō chased after him, and caught him by his elbows, swinging him around four or five times. Kasuke got a mouthful of water. He spat it out and began coughing.

"I quit. I'm not playing anymore," Kasuke said.

The other children went to stand up on the gravelly bank. Saburō stood alone beneath the honey locust tree.

By then, the sky had filled with black clouds. The willow tree seemed to turn white and the mountain grasses darkened, making everything look eerie. Thunder rang out in the upper fields. There was a sound like a tidal wave, and then all at once it began to rain and the wind started blowing. Large drops of water the size of rocks splashed into the swimming hole. The children grabbed their clothes from the river bank and ran for cover underneath the silk tree. Saburō became frightened and dove into the water from beneath the honey locust tree and swam toward the others.

A mysterious voice called out from the sky,

Let the rain pour down,
Amesaburo!
Let the wind blow hard,
Matasaburo!

The boys sang together,

Let the rain pour down,

Amesaburo!
Let the wind blow hard,
Matasaburo!

Saburō hurriedly jumped up out of the swimming hole as if something were going to grab his feet and ran at full speed toward the other boys. Trembling, he asked, "Was that you guys who just said that?"

"No! No!" everyone vigorously denied.

"No!" Pekichi chimed in.

Looking toward the river and biting his pale lips, Saburō asked, "What's going on?" His body trembled uncontrollably.

Everyone waited for the rain to stop and then returned home.

September 12: The Twelfth Day

doh dohdoh dohdohhdoh . . .
Blow away the green walnuts,
and the sour quinces too!
doh dohdoh dohdohhdoh . . .

In a dream, Ichirō heard the poem that he had heard from Saburō several days before. He awoke with a start. The wind was blowing fiercely, making the woods howl. The pale darkness of the approaching dawn rested on the screen door, on the tops of the shelves, on the lamp shade, and on the entire house. Ichirō quickly tied his sash and put on his shoes. Passing in front of the stable, he went to the door and opened it. Wind and cold drops of rain came blowing in. At the back of the stable, a door was clattering, which made the horses cry out.

Drawing in a deep breath, Ichirō felt the wind soak into the core of his chest. It was almost light outside and the ground was wet. The row of chestnut trees in front of the house, which had a strange bluish-white hue, whipped back and forth in the wind and the rain as if they were being laundered. Green leaves were strewn about, and chestnut burrs had been blown off the trees and had fallen onto the black ground.

The clouds glared an angry gray and moved rapidly toward the north. The distant wood was suddenly filled with a crashing sound, as of a raging sea. Big cold raindrops fell on Ichirō's face and the wind blew so hard that it seemed as if his clothes were going to be ripped off. He listened to the sounds around him as he looked intently up into the sky. He felt a great pressure in his chest, and as he continued to listen to the howling of the wind, his heart began pounding.

Until today, the scenery had been motionless and the wind had been silent. But this morning, everything suddenly started moving. Ichirō guessed that the wind was blowing toward the northern end of the Tuscarora seabed.

Ichirō's face became hot and his breath heavy. He felt as if he were going to fly up into the sky. He inhaled deeply and filled his chest with air.

"What a terrible wind. The tobacco and the millet will be completely destroyed today," said Ichirō's grandfather, who was standing in the doorway looking up at the sky.

Ichirō hurriedly got a bucketful of water from the well and washed the kitchen floor. He got out the basin and scrubbed his face, and then took out some cold rice and bean paste from the cabinet. He ate quickly, as if he were in a trance.

"Ichirō, wait a minute. The soup will be ready soon. Do you have to go to school early today?" his mother asked, as she put wood on the kitchen stove where they cooked the food for the horses.

"Yes. Matasaburō might have flown away."

"Is Matasaburō a bird?"

"No, he's a person." Ichirō said. He hurriedly put away the rice and washed his bowl as soon as he finished eating. He put on his raincoat, which was hanging from a nail on the wall, and took off his shoes, and then ran barefoot to meet Kasuke. Kasuke, who had just gotten up, called out, "I'm just going to eat breakfast now."

Ichirō waited impatiently in front of the barn. Kasuke soon came out, wearing a little straw raincoat.

The two boys trudged through the violent rain and finally arrived at school, completely soaked. They went inside and found the classroom still empty. Here and there, through the holes in the windows, rain fell on the floor.

Ichirō glanced around the classroom and said, "Kasuke, the two of us should mop the floor."

Ichirō got a mop and began mopping beneath a window. Hearing noises, the teacher came out to see who had arrived. He wore regular clothes and held a red fan in his hand.

"It's very early. Are you two cleaning the classroom?" asked the teacher.

"Good morning, teacher," Ichirō said.

"Good morning, teacher," said Kasuke, and then immediately asked, "Teacher, is Matasaburō coming in today?"

The teacher thought for a moment and then asked, "When you say Matasaburō, do you mean Mr. Takada? Well, actually, Mr. Takada went away yesterday with his father. It was Sunday, so he wasn't able to say goodbye to everyone."

"Did he fly away?" Kasuke asked.

"No, his father got a telegram from his company, calling him back. His father may return here again, but Mr. Takada will go to school up there. His mother is there."

"Why did his company call him?" Ichirō asked.

"Because the mining for the molybdenum deposit will not start for a while."

"I don't believe it. He really was Matasaburō of the wind after all!" Kasuke yelled loudly.

A sound came from the back of the schoolhouse. The teacher, holding his red fan, rushed to see what it was.

The two boys stood facing each other for a while without saying anything, as if each were trying to figure out what the other was really thinking.

The wind kept blowing and the windows rattled as they became clouded with raindrops.

A BUNCH OF GRAPES

Arishima Takeo

When I was little, I liked to paint pictures. I went to school in a place called Yamanote in Yokohama. It was a town where only foreigners lived, and in my school there were only foreign teachers. On the way to and from school, I used to walk down a street by the sea that was lined with hotels and Western companies. If I stood at the shore, I could see many warships and merchant boats lined up on the deep blue sea. Smoke billowed from the smokestacks, and flags draped between the masts. It was so beautiful it almost made my eyes hurt. I often stood on the bank to admire this view, and when I returned home, I tried to paint what I saw as faithfully as I could, but with the paints that I had, as hard as I tried, I couldn't seem to capture the seemingly transparent blue of the sea and the crimson painted near the waterline of the white sailing ships. No matter how many times I painted it, I couldn't match the colors of the actual scene.

I remembered the set of Western paints that belonged to a friend at school. This friend was, of course, a foreigner and because he was two years older than me, he was so tall I had to look up at him. His name was Jim, and the paints he had were high-quality imports. Inside a lightweight wooden box, the twelve colors of paint were arranged in two rows of hardened squares like small blocks of sumi ink. Every color was exquisite, but the blue and red were especially breathtaking. Though Jim was taller than me, he was a far worse painter. Even so, using those paints, even the worst pictures seemed to be transformed into ones of such beauty that you couldn't believe your eyes. I was always jealous of that. Resentful

of my own poor-quality paints, I imagined that if I had paints like Jim's, I could paint the ocean the way it really looked. From that day on, I wanted Jim's paints so badly that I couldn't stand it, but was ashamed to ask mother or father to buy some for me. I therefore continued to think about those paints for many days.

I can't remember exactly when it was, but it must have been autumn because the grapes were ripe. It was a day like so many before the arrival of winter, so clear that the sky seemed limitless. I ate lunch with my teacher, but even in the middle of break time, my heart was somewhat restless and was as cloudy as the sun was bright. I was lost in my own thoughts. If someone had looked carefully, they might have noticed that my face was pale. I wanted Jim's paints so badly I couldn't stand it. I wanted them so badly my chest hurt. I thought for sure that Jim knew what I was wishing, but when I sneaked a glance at his face, he was smiling as if he knew nothing, chatting with the students sitting next to him. But to me it seemed he was smiling because he knew my secret, and I could have sworn he was telling his friends, "Keep your eyes on that Japanese guy. He's going to steal my paints." I was miserable. The more Jim seemed to suspect me, the more I wanted his paints.

I may have had a charming enough face, but I was weak in both body and spirit. On top of that, I was shy, and it was in my nature not to speak my mind. For this reason, I was not very popular and had few friends. When lunch time was over, the other kids went dashing out to the playground and ran around playing, but I sat by myself in the classroom, more sullen than usual that day. Although it was bright outside, the classroom was as dark as the depths of my heart.

As I sat there, my eyes occasionally fell on Jim's desk. The top had lots of graffiti carved into it with a knife and had turned black from use. I opened it. Inside, along with books and notebooks and writing plates, was the shiny, honey-colored paint box. Inside that box were blue and red paints in the shape of sumi ink blocks. I felt my face becoming hot and looked away. But I couldn't help glancing at Jim's desk again. My heart beat quickly and I felt smothered. Sitting still, I panicked. I felt the way I feel when I am being chased by a monster in a dream.

The bell rang to call the students back to the classroom. Startled, I stood up involuntarily. Through the window I could see the students going to the sink to wash their hands, laughing and hollering. Aware of an iciness inside my head, I suddenly staggered over to Jim's desk and, half in a dream, lifted the top. As I expected, the familiar paint box was stashed away in the desk, along with notebooks and a pencil case. For some stupid reason, after glancing around me, I lifted the top of the box and quickly took the blue and the red paints and stuffed them into my pocket. I then hurriedly ran over to the place where we line up to wait for the teacher.

We were led into the classroom by the young teacher, and we sat down in our seats. I wanted badly to see Jim's expression, but couldn't bring myself to look in his direction. Nobody seemed to notice what I had done, and I was left with an uneasy sense of relief in my heart. Though I could hear the pleasant voice of the young teacher whom I liked so much, for some reason I couldn't

make out anything she said. It seemed to me that she looked at me quizzically from time to time, but that day, I just couldn't bring myself to look her in the eye. I avoided her glances for the entire hour. I just sat there thinking that everyone was whispering behind my back.

The bell rang to leave the classroom and I heaved a sigh of relief. But when the teacher left, the biggest and smartest student in the class grabbed my elbow and said, "Come here for a second."

My chest began to tremble involuntarily, the way it did when the teacher called on me and I hadn't done my homework. I was determined to act as casual as possible, so with a nonchalant expression, I let myself be led to the corner of the playground.

"You've got Jim's paints. Give them to me," he said.

The student thrust his hand toward me, palm up. Instead of coming clean, I calmly lied by blurting out, "I don't have them."

Jim approached me with three or four of his friends. His voice trembling a little, he said, "I checked my paint box before the lunch break. Not one was missing. But afterward, two were missing and you were the only one in the classroom."

I knew that this was the end. I felt blood rushing to my head, and my face turned red. Someone tried to stick his hand in my pocket. I resisted vigorously, but to no avail, for I was outnumbered. In front of everyone, along with some "marbles" (or "B balls," as they are called today), pencils, and playing cards, he grabbed the two blocks of paint. The expression on his face said, "Aha!" and the other kids stared at me in disgust. My body shook uncontrollably and everything seemed to go black. In the midst of such fine weather, despite the fact that my fellow students were playing happily around me, I became helplessly downhearted. How could I have done such a thing? I couldn't undo it. I was doomed. With these thoughts in my head, I began to feel lonely and sad, and finally burst into tears.

"You can't get away with it by crying," said the clever, brawny kid in a mocking, hateful tone. I refused to budge as they tried to drag me to the second floor. I resisted as much as possible but was overpowered and dragged up the stairs to the office of the homeroom teacher I liked so much.

Jim knocked on the door. From inside, we could hear the teacher kindly beckoning us inside. I have never felt as awful as I did when I entered that room.

The teacher, who was writing, seemed a little startled when she saw us all pour into the room. With her right hand she stroked her hair, which was chopped off at the neck like a man's. She turned her always-sweet face toward us and tilted her head a little as if to ask what we wanted. Then the clever, brawny kid stepped forward and explained in detail about my taking Jim's paints. The teacher, with a slightly confused expression, looked around at everyone and then at my half-crying face. She asked me if this was true. Although it was in fact true, I just couldn't bring myself to admit to the teacher I liked so much that I was such a bad person—so instead of answering, I burst out crying.

The teacher looked at me for a while, then at the students, and said quietly, "You may leave now." All the other students, a little taken aback, went downstairs in a commotion.

The teacher, without saying anything, without even facing me, looked at her fingernails for a while. Soon she stood up quietly and came over and put her arm around me. In a low voice, she asked, "Did you return the paints already?" Because I wanted the teacher to know without a doubt that I had, I nodded very deeply.

"Do you think what you did was wrong?"

When the teacher gently repeated the question one more time, I couldn't stand it anymore. I trembled violently, and though I tried biting my lip, I cried out and tears flooded from my eyes. I wanted to die right then and there in the teacher's arms.

"Don't cry anymore. As long as you understand that what you did was wrong, let's leave it at that. Stop crying, okay? During the next period, you don't have to go to the classroom. Stay in my office and settle down. Stay here until I come back, okay?" she said as she sat me on the couch.

The study bell rang, and she took her notes from on top of her desk and looked at me. She broke off a bunch of grapes from the grapevine that had grown up to the second-floor window and put them on my lap. As I continued to cry, she quietly left the room.

The noisy students went into the classroom and suddenly everything became silent. I grew hopelessly sad. When I thought about the fact that I had brought suffering to the teacher whom I liked, I realized that I had done something truly wrong. I didn't feel like eating the grapes at all and continued to cry.

Suddenly, I felt my shoulders being shaken lightly and woke up. It seems that I had cried myself to sleep. The teacher, who was slightly lanky, was smiling and looking down at me. Because I had fallen asleep, I had forgotten what had happened and I felt fine. I laughed nervously and quickly picked up the bunch of grapes that were about to fall off my lap, but I suddenly remembered the sad incident and my good spirits disappeared.

"You look so sad. Everyone has gone home. You go home too. But no matter what, you must come to school tomorrow. If I don't see your face, I'll be sad," the teacher said and gently put the bunch of grapes in my bag. Feeling gloomy, I went home along the shore road as usual, gazing at the ocean and the boats, and ate all the delicious grapes.

The next day, I didn't feel like going to school. I wished my stomach or my head would begin to hurt, but that day I didn't even feel the ache of a single cavity. There was nothing I could do, so I reluctantly left the house and slowly made my way to school, deep in thought. Arriving at the gate, I couldn't bring myself to go in. But then I remembered my teacher's parting words. All I wanted to do was see my teacher's face. If I didn't go, the teacher would surely be disappointed. I wanted the teacher to look at me with her kind eyes one more time. With that as my only motivation, I went through the gate.

To my surprise, Jim came rushing toward me and took my hand as if he had been waiting for me. It seemed as if he had forgotten what had happened the day before, and he kindly led me to the teacher's office. I was very confused. I had imagined that when I got to school, everyone would be staring at me across the yard, saying things like, "Look at that lying Japanese thief." Being treated like this made me feel guilty.

As if she had heard our footsteps, the teacher opened the door before Jim knocked, and we both entered.

"Jim, you are a good boy. You understood what I explained to you." She turned to me. "Jim has already said that you do not have to apologize to him. If from now on you two can be good friends, that's enough. Now shake hands," the teacher said with a smile as she turned us to face each other. As I stood there looking self-conscious and awkward, Jim grabbed my hand, which was dangling at my side, and held it firmly. I didn't know how to express my happiness so I just laughed nervously. Jim was also smiling kindly. The teacher asked me, "Did you like the grapes I gave you yesterday?"

"Yes," I confessed, turning bright red.

"Well then, I'll give you some more," she said. Dressed from head to toe in white linen, she stretched out the window, grabbed a bunch, and put the powdered purple grapes on the white palm of her left hand. Then, with a pair of long silver scissors, she cut the bunch down the middle and handed the grapes to Jim and me. I can still remember how beautiful the purple grapes looked sitting on her pure white palm.

From that day on, I was a little better behaved than before, and a little less shy.

Where is that teacher I liked so much? I know that I'll never see her again, but still keep wishing that I could. When autumn comes, the grapes turn purple and become coated with a beautiful powder, but the lovely, marble-like, white hand that held them is nowhere to be found.

THE MOONLIT NIGHT AND THE EYEGLASSES

Ogawa Mimei

It was around the time of year when the towns and the fields are all covered with green leaves.

It happened on a peaceful night with a fine moon. On the outskirts of a quiet town, an old woman was sitting all alone next to her window doing needlework. A lamp cast a peaceful glow all around her. As the woman was already quite old, her eyesight had grown dim, and she had trouble getting her thread to pass through the eye of her needle. She held the needle up to the lamp over and over again, and twisted the thin thread with her wrinkled fingertips.

The moon shed a pale light over this world. The groves, the houses, and the hills appeared to be soaked in its warm water. While the old woman was working, she daydreamed about her youth, about her distant relatives, about her granddaughter who lived in another village, and about other things. It was quiet all around, and the only sound was the *tick tock, tick tock* of the alarm clock on the shelf. Every once in a while, the voice of a street vendor out on the crowded, bustling street, or the faint rumbling of a passing train could be heard.

The old woman could scarcely remember where she was or what she was doing, and was sitting absent-mindedly, feeling peaceful as if she were having a dream. Just then, there was a *knock knock* at the front door. The old woman leaned a near-deaf ear in the direction of the sound. She wasn't expecting anyone to come visiting at this hour. Surely it was the sound of the wind, she thought, the way it passes aimlessly through the fields and villages. Then

came the sound of little footsteps just under the window. Strangely, the old woman was able to hear this sound.

"Ma'am. Excuse me, ma'am!" somebody called out.

At first the old woman thought she must be hearing things, and stopped moving her hands.

"Ma'am, please open the window," somebody said again.

"Who could be saying this?" the woman wondered, and she got up and opened the window. Outside, it was as bright as day by the blue-white light of the moon.

Under the window stood a not very tall man. He was looking up at her through black-rimmed eyeglasses, and, he had a beard.

"I don't know you. Who are you?" said the old woman. She looked at the face of the unfamiliar man, and thought that this person had somehow made a mistake and come to the wrong house.

"I am an eyeglass salesman. I have many different kinds of eyeglasses. Although this is the first time I have been to this village, it is truly pleasant and beautiful. There is a fine moon, an ideal night to vend my wares," said the man.

The old woman, having only just a few moments before had trouble threading her needle because of her eyesight, asked, "Do you have eyeglasses that would suit my eyes and make me see well?"

The man opened the lid of the box that he was carrying and poked around for a pair of glasses that would suit her. He soon pulled out a large pair of glasses with tortoise-shell frames and handed them to the old woman through the window.

"I guarantee that with these you will be able to see everything clearly," he said. All around him, as he stood under the window, bloomed many white, crimson, and blue flowers, giving off a sweet scent.

The old woman put on the glasses and tried to read the numbers on the alarm clock across the room and the letters on the calendar. She could see each and every character perfectly! She remembered that, decades ago, as a young girl, she had been able to see this clearly. She was overjoyed.

"I'll take them!" she said, and promptly bought the glasses.

After the old woman made her purchase, the salesman with the black-rimmed glasses and the beard went on his way. When the man had passed out of sight, the flowers continued to give off their fragrance into the night air.

The old woman closed the window and sat back down where she had been before. Now she could thread her needle without any trouble at all. She put on and took off her eyeglasses over and over again. She was filled with a childlike curiosity and wanted to look at all the things around her. Since she was not used to wearing the glasses, she was thrilled by the sudden change in her surroundings every time she put them on.

The old woman took off the eyeglasses once more. She placed

them near the alarm clock on the shelf, and thinking that the hour had gotten quite late and that she should go to bed, started putting her needlework away.

Just then, there was a *tap tap* at the front door. The old woman leaned over to listen.

"What a strange evening this is," the old woman said. "It seems that someone has come again. And at such a. . . ." When she looked at the clock, although the light of the moon made it bright outside, the hour was very late.

The old woman got up and walked toward the front door. It appeared that someone with small hands was knocking, making a faint *tap tap* sound.

"At this late hour . . ." the old woman muttered as she opened the front door. A beautiful girl of about twelve or thirteen was standing there. She had long hair and her eyes were full of tears.

"Who are you and why have you come visiting so late?" the old woman asked suspiciously.

"I work for the village perfume factory. Day after day I fill bottles with perfume taken from white roses, and then I go home late at night. I worked tonight too, and since there is a fine moon, I took a stroll by myself, and I tripped over a rock and I cut my finger. It hurts so much I can't bear it. It's bleeding and it won't stop. The people in all of the houses have already gone to sleep. As I passed in front of this house, I saw that you were still awake. I know that you are kind and gentle and a good person, so I finally brought myself to knock on your door," said the beautiful little girl.

The old woman noticed that the little girl's body was scented with fine perfume, and as they talked, the aroma drifted up to her nose.

"Then, you know who I am?" asked the old woman.

"I know you because I have passed in front of this house many times and have seen you sitting by the window doing needlework," answered the little girl.

"There's a good girl. Which one, show me your hurt finger. Let's put some medicine on it," said the old woman as she brought

the girl over to the lamp. The little girl stuck out her little hand. Red blood flowed from her finger.

"How sad. She cut it on a rock," the old woman muttered, but because her eyesight was dim, she couldn't really tell where the blood was coming from.

"Where did I put those eyeglasses I just got?" the old woman said as she searched the shelf. Finding the glasses near the alarm clock, she immediately put them on so she could see the little girl's wound.

Wearing her eyeglasses, the old woman tried to get a good look at the face of the beautiful young girl who said she had passed in front of her house many times. She was startled by what she saw—not a young girl but a pretty butterfly. The old woman remembered a story she had once heard about butterflies taking the shape of people on peaceful moonlit nights and visiting houses where people were up late at night. This butterfly had hurt its leg.

"There's a good girl. Come with me," the old woman said kindly. She stood up and went out the door and around to the flower garden behind the house. The little girl silently followed the old woman.

In the garden, all the flowers were blooming as if they knew it was their time to peak. During the day, butterflies graced the garden and honey bees bustled about, but now they seemed to be resting in the shade of the leaves, dreaming happy dreams. The garden was completely quiet, and the pale light of the moon flowed over it like water. On the fence at the far end of the garden, wild white roses were huddled together blooming like snow.

"I wonder where she went," said the old woman, stopping suddenly to look back. The little girl who was following her had disappeared unnoticed, without so much as the sound of a footstep, and was nowhere in sight.

"Good night, everyone. I'm going to sleep now too," said the old woman and went inside the house.

It truly was a splendid moonlit night.

A RAINBOW IN THE DESERT

Tsubotā Joji

There once was a large field. Not one tree or blade of grass was growing on it. Beyond the field there was a mountain range. There were many mountains stretching far into the distance as far as the eye could see. On this grassless field and in these treeless mountains where no animals could survive, there lived not so much as one single mouse or insect. From time to time, the wind would come down from the sky to blow up a dust cloud, playfully running this way and that. But that was all. When night fell, the moon quietly cast its beams from behind the jagged stones of the bare mountains, gazing down on this world. Perhaps the moon was thinking, "What a desolate place, frightfully desolate."

Something happened one day in the summer of a certain year. Shimmering silver clouds blanketed this lonely world. The peaked clouds floated up into the sky, taking the shapes of high towers, huge monsters, and Buddhas sitting on lotus flowers. The land was so barren and the sky was so beautiful that had there been a single human being living in this desert, he would surely have thought, "This must be the beginning of a festival in the heavens."

The festival in the heavens went on for three days. On the fourth day, rain began pounding down on the desert, something that had not happened for many years. The rain did not slow down, even for a minute. In fact, it rained for seven days and seven nights. Even though it rained this much, there was no flood, because this land had not seen rain for many years. All the water was sucked down through the soil into the depths of the earth.

After seven days, the rain stopped and something curious hap-

pened. In a valley of the desert mountain range, where trees and grass did not grow, a huge rainbow appeared. From halfway up one mountain to the very top of another one far away, the rainbow painted a five-colored bridge across the sky. This rainbow was all the more marvelous and beautiful because it appeared in a mountain range where neither man nor beast, bird nor insect, not even one single fish was living. It remained for three days, through both the days and the nights.

On the morning of the fourth day the rainbow was gone. It had disappeared during the previous night. When the sun crept cautiously out from behind the mountain, dreading the sight of the frighteningly lonely valley, it was pleasantly surprised. A large tree stood halfway up the mountain, where the base of the rainbow had been. The tree was many, many meters high and more than ten meters wide. Moreover, countless numbers of flowers were growing on each of the large limbs that extended in all directions, and on each of the many small limbs. The petals were delicate and red like those of the cherry blossom, but as big as those of the lotus. It seemed as if a forest of flowers was in bloom on this one tree. The morning sun was startled as it cast its rays from behind the mountain onto the flowering tree.

In the afternoon, the sun shone ever-stronger rays on the valley. The stronger the rays got, the more beautifully the flowering tree sparkled, giving off an indescribably delicious scent which seemed to rise into the sky like a violet haze.

In the afternoon, the late-day sun cast its light on the western mountains. As the valleys and mountains were dyed in the colors of sunset, a wind blew down into the valley of the blossoming tree. It was not the kind of strong wind that would blow up dust clouds, but the flowers on the flowering tree were blown off and scattered all the same. At first only three or four flowers fell, but soon the air turned white, as in a snowstorm. The petals formed one huge mass, falling in a single white flow. They danced in the sky as they scattered about the valley. Some of the petals got caught on the tops of mountains, while others cleared the mountain tops and landed in a far valley. When the evening light faded from the tops of the mountains, the flowering tree stood naked. All its branches were bare.

The next day, the morning sun peeked cautiously once more from behind the mountains into the valley where the flowering tree stood. It was probably thinking, "Yesterday the wind mercilessly blew the flowers off the tree. I wonder how the tree looks and feels today." It aimed its rays into the valley and saw a pleasing sight. Though the flowers on the flowering tree had fallen off and not one branch had a flower remaining on it, the entire tree—all the branches and even the trunk—was completely hidden by a thick layer of green leaves that rustled coolly in the breeze. The morning sun was probably saying to himself, "I'm so relieved. There's no need for me to worry anymore."

From that day on, the tree stood firm. Even if it was blown by the wind, it did not shed its leaves, and it remained green and lush for a long time.

Many years later, a beautiful spring appeared, gushing out from beneath a big rock at the foot of the tree. Come summertime, even autumn, the spring did not dry up. It continued to rush forth without ever stopping. The spring soon became a small river. The river ran down the side of the mountain and flowed into a valley. It flowed through the valley into another valley, and after twisting and turning many times, it flowed into the field. It flowed endlessly through the wide field and on beyond the horizon. It probably ended up reaching the sea.

More years passed. Trees began popping up at the banks of the little river. They grew up to be strong and sprouted many flowers and leaves. They were tall like Japanese cedars, and they grew in all parts of the valley, wherever their seeds were blown around by the wind.

One day, a bird came flying from some unknown place. It was a white bird. Feathers grew on its head like a crown, and its tail fluttered like three ribbons. The bird lit on the top branch of a tree that stood on the bank of the small river in the valley. *"Kwaa kwa kwa kwa,"* it called out. From beyond the sky came many such birds, flying with their tail feathers fluttering. Not just white birds, but birds with gold feathers, bright red feathers, and even purple feathers. They were probably Chinese Phoenixes. When they perched on the trees in the valley, they looked like beautiful flowers. As the Phoenixes spread their white or red blossomlike wings, they jumped from tree to tree and danced up into the sky above the valley, flying higher than the clouds. When they flew from one tree to another, it seemed as though they were pulling thick gold or purple threads behind them, and when they soared high up into the sky, they looked like flower petals being blown by the wind.

After the birds came to live in the trees of the valley, the water in the spring gradually began to rise. This might have been because it started raining often, or it might have been because the water was called forth by the voices of the birds exchanging greetings. For whatever reason, the water began flowing vigorously. The river grew wider and wider. Midway along its course, a ledge formed, and the ledge became a big flowing waterfall that gave off a lot of spray. Needless to say, the area downstream from the waterfall became much broader and deeper until finally, in the middle of the field, there was a big lake.

After that, again many years passed. Then something else mysterious occurred. At some unknown time, a big toad began living near the spring. It was three meters tall and looked like a huge boulder. When it saw something unfamiliar, the toad crouched quietly near the spring, still as a rock.

Why did it do this?

The toad was a water god who was there to guard against creatures who muddied and dirtied the water.

The valley soon became crowded with creatures. Endless numbers of them came to drink water at the spring, and the toad gobbled them up one after another. Among the creatures were salmon and trout from the sea who yearned for the beautifully cold, sweet waters that flowed from the spring. They swam upstream against the spray of the waterfall every year to lay their eggs, and the toad, who was waiting for them, would gobble them up. Over the years the toad grew bigger and bigger until finally, still looking like a boulder, it was over ten meters high.

Then the rains stopped. Many years passed without rain. The water in the spring gradually began to dry up. Before long the river in the valley became narrow and the grass and trees began to wither. The creatures in the valley disappeared. No one knows where they went. The toad near the spring began wasting away. Soon it was nothing but skin and bones. The wind would come and playfully blow up dust clouds. The valley reverted to the desert it had been long ago.

One year, just as it had happened years before, peaked silver clouds blanketed the desert. Clouds in the shape of towers, huge monsters, and Buddhas sitting on lotus flowers lined up against the sky. Then it rained again. When the rain stopped, a rainbow appeared. The rainbow spread over the gloomy desert valley and remained there night and day for three days. There were no grasses and no trees, there was no spring and no river, there were no creatures, and there was no toad. The whole valley was covered in a layer of gray dust. Not one person came passing through, and the desert rainbow knew no one.

Before long, the rainbow disappeared. After that, for hundreds of years, no rainbow rose up to arch over the valley again.

THE ONION CLUB

Hayashi Fumiko

Shige Ōki, Kōtarō Namekawa, Gan Katagai, and Zen Okudaira. These are the members of the Onion Club.

The person who gave the Onion Club its name was Shōsaku, Gan's older brother. The four boys were great friends. They were also very emotional and were moved to tears by just about anything. Shōsaku named them the "Onion Club" because they would cry for almost any reason. Shige was a sixth-grader, Kō and Zen were in their first year at Public Junior High School X, and Gan was in his first year at XX Business Middle School.

Before the air raids, they all lived on X street in Kōjimachi. During the air raids, the neighborhood was burned and the four were separated. They found each other after the war and started meeting again.

Shige was staying at his uncle's house in Mitaka. Kō was living with his older sister's husband's family in Kamakura Yukinoshita. Gan's family was renting a house on Kotaki street in Nakano.

No one in the families of these three boys was harmed, but Zen's father died fighting in Burma and his mother became sick and died in Kofu, where she had been evacuated to. Zen returned to Tokyo with his older sister, and they lived with their uncle in Ikegami.

The club decided to meet once a month at Gan's house on Kotaki Street. Shōsaku used to tease them by saying that when the four of them got together in the small house, it was as noisy as a festival, or it sounded as if there were ten radios going at once.

Since the Onion Club met only once a month, the members

decided that, between meetings, each of them was to do something great and report back to the club about it. But according to Zen, the point was not to deliberately go out and do something great. "To do something great" meant, by Zen's definition, to do it spontaneously. Therefore, by Zen's definition, if you didn't do something great, so be it. Everyone agreed with Zen's definition.

Gan, however, was fond of adventure and had a wild imagination. The members of the Onion Club nicknamed him Gan the Dreamer. The September meeting was coming up, and Gan the Dreamer was scheming for a chance to do something great.

It was Sunday. Gan finished his homework, stuffed two rolls that his mother had made for him into his pocket, and went out the door. He wondered if there was something great to be done. He was thinking that he'd like to do something so great that it would make the club members gasp.

As he wandered over to Shinjuku Station, everything he saw and heard seemed to offer interesting possibilities. A human river flowed through the station. As he watched the waves of people going by, Gan's appetite for adventure grew bigger and bigger. In front of the station, as people swarmed around him, he saw two blind men wearing dark glasses holding hands tightly and wandering around as if being tossed by the human waves. They were carrying big backpacks and bamboo sticks. As Gan stared at them, the two bewildered men came to a standstill in the middle of the station hall. Seeing them whisper to each other, Gan went over to them and asked, "Where are you going?"

The blind men seemed a little startled to hear a child's voice. "We are going to Ueno. We can't figure out where to buy tickets," they said, turning left and right.

"Well then, I'll go buy them for you," Gan said.

The blind men tilted their heads doubtfully and made no move to get out their money. Sensing their suspicion, Gan said, "Stay here. I have money. I'll go get them," and went to buy three tickets.

"Here are your tickets. I'll go with you as far as Ueno," Gan said and put two tickets in the men's hands. The men were embarrassed and took out their wallets.

"It's okay. You might get your wallet stolen by a pickpocket here. Let's just go," Gan said.

Gan took one of them by the hand and headed for the ticket gate. When they got to the Chuo line, the blind men thanked him many times.

"Where are you going from Ueno?" Gan asked.

"We're going to Nagano, and from there we're going to a hot springs town called Yutanaka to find work giving massages."

"Oh, that's far away, and a lot of trouble to get to."

"Where are you from, young man?"

"I used to live in Kojimachi, but it burned down. For half a year, I was relocated to Kusatsu with my mother and family."

"What's it like in Kusatsu? Are the inns doing good business?"

"Well, I was staying with family friends, so I really wouldn't know. The inns were full, but mostly with evacuated students, so I'm not sure if they're doing all that well."

The train came and the three of them got on with some difficulty.

"Thank you so much for your help," the two blind men said. They seemed extremely relieved.

"After we reach Ueno, I'll take you to the waiting area for the 2:15 train to Niigata," said Gan.

"In all my years, I've never met anyone as kind as you," said the taller of the blind men, smiling with delight.

"Were you a soldier?" asked Gan.

"I was in Manchuria for a long time, and from there I went to China, where I was blinded," he said.

"So, he was a soldier," thought Gan, feeling sorry for the man. He realized that he was really doing something great that day.

When they arrived at Ueno again, there were enormous waves of people. Gan finally found the line for the Niigata-bound train, but there were already a lot of people waiting. Even so, it was more than two hours before the train would depart and it seemed that the blind men would be able to get on. They would probably have a hard time once they passed through the ticket puncher's gate, though. Gan tried to figure out what to do.

"Once you get your ticket punched, the other people will all run onto the train, so it will be difficult. I'll sneak past the ticket gate over there and get you on the train," he said.

The blind men responded, "No, that would be too much bother. If you're caught by the station worker and get in trouble it would be terrible."

They were worried.

When they got on line at the ticket gate, the two men finally put down their backpacks and heaved a sigh of relief. They explained to him that because they didn't have a place to live in Tokyo and they didn't have many customers, they were going to do the rounds of the hot springs resorts in Nagano. There were unions at the hot springs and it was hard to get in, but they planned to settle there

and somehow work to make ends meet. Things were expensive wherever they went and it was difficult to find food. Not having been born blind, they were truly handicapped by blindness and there was nothing they could do about it. The shorter one grumbled that his eyes went bad when he was about twelve or thirteen and that he had a very hard time.

"I want to smoke a cigarette, but I haven't had one in four days. Corona and Peace are expensive and I can't buy them. My head is spinning," he said. The one who said he was a soldier laughed sadly.

There was still plenty of time, so Gan left them where they

were and went to investigate the possibility of sneaking onto the platform. The platform was empty now. To the right, there was a ticket gate where station employees were going in and out.

I've got to get in there and get those two on the train, thought Gan. He lingered around the gate for a while. His heart beat faster and faster. He wondered if he could slip in unnoticed like a plume of smoke.

The ticket gate began to seem menacing like a locked fortress. Gan wished he had the power to shrink down to the size of a mouse.

While Gan was scheming by the gate, an American soldier quickly jumped over the ticket gate and went onto the platform. If only he were fluent in English, he could ask the soldier to look after the two blind men, he thought. But what could he do? It wasn't as if he could just start looking up words in English right there on the spot.

Just then, a kind-looking female station worker came to the ticket gate. Gan was startled and moved away from the gate. He suddenly remembered the lesson on equality that he learned in school, and thought that he could perhaps ask her to help him with the blind men. He blushed and said, "Ummm. . . ," as he approached her with hesitation. He tried to tell her everything that had happened to him at Shinjuku Station, but the woman would not listen to his story and, without a word, walked quickly away.

Gan was nearly in tears. He didn't know what to do and felt hopeless. "I'm long-winded and not very good at telling stories," he thought. He had to figure out a way to get through the ticket gate.

He waded through the crowd and as he returned to where the blind men were, he saw that they were splitting a black roll. It appeared that they had only one roll between the two of them, so Gan took out the two rolls he had brought from home and gave the blind men one each.

"No, we'll make do. It's okay. You're hungry too, aren't you? We really can't accept these. . . ."

The line was gradually getting longer. Gan forced the bread into their hands and said, "Mine are made with American flour, so they taste good. When I go home I can get some more."

The blind men held the rolls on their palms and bowed politely with great delight. The people in the crowd around them seemed sympathetic to the blind men, but Gan knew very well that when the ticket punching began, their sympathy would disappear.

The time came to take tickets and the blind men hurriedly put on their backpacks. Gan's adventure began.

As soon as the ticket taking started, Gan slipped onto the platform from the place he had staked out earlier. He felt as if he had been blessed by the gods. At the ticket gate where the crowds were rushing forward, he found the two men being pushed back and forth. Gan pulled them to the train and pushed them through the window by their backsides.

"Well, you should be okay now. Good-bye. Take care of yourselves." Gan said.

When Gan shook their hands, the blind man who had been a soldier said, "Please take this." He gave Gan a Braille newspaper, which Gan gladly accepted.

There were still many people pouring onto the platform. Gan was famished. He went out to the front of the station into the bright sunlight and spread out the newspaper. There were four 50-sen bills inside. Gan put the wrinkled, dirty bills in his pocket. He was really hungry, so he hurried home.

The day came for the Onion Club meeting. For some reason the usually high-spirited Gan did not speak of taking the blind men to Ueno Station. It seemed somehow wrong to boast about it as if it were an especially great thing he had done.

"Gan, did something happen?" asked Zen.

"No. Nothing particularly exciting happened."

As he said this, Gan the Dreamer closed his eyes and touched the tattered Braille newspaper with his finger. The other boys stared at it in wonder.

KUMA

Shiga Naoya

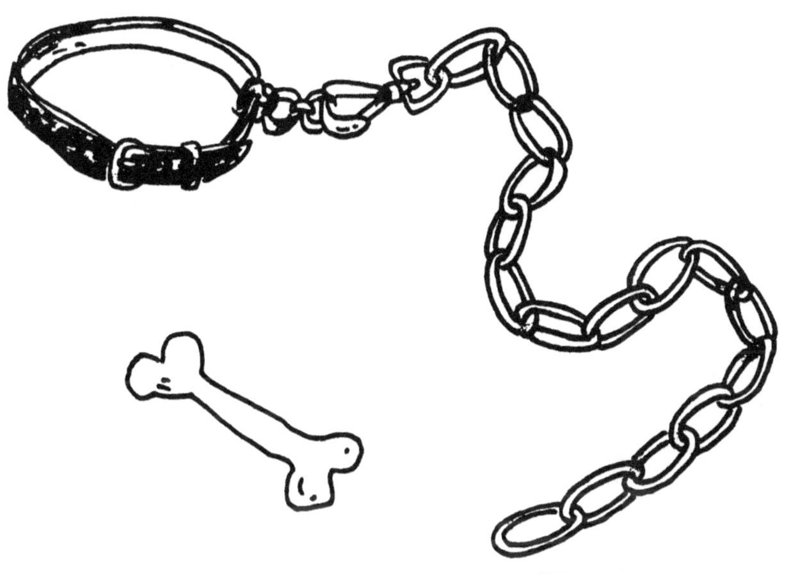

Naka was the greyhound that was given to me years ago by my friend, Mr. Tanizaki of Okamoto. He was also the rather handsome dog in the novel *Some Prefer Nettles,* and he appeared in the illustrations of my friend, the late Mr. Narashiga Koide. Naka grew old and sick. I had been thinking he would not be with us for much longer, and then I was awoken one morning by the alarmed voices of my wife and children. Their voices came from in front of my bedroom, and I knew right then and there that Naka was dead.

At that time, I was suffering from gallstones and was weary, body and soul. I also didn't much feel like seeing Naka's lifeless face. Therefore, without getting up, I told my wife to call the handyman from Hyakugōji village and have him bury the dog out there, and I didn't get out of bed at all.

It seemed to me that it was not by mere chance, but due to a profound attachment, that Naka had collapsed not two meters from my pillow.

Ever since I was a child, I had liked to raise animals, and I had always had pets. But as I grew older—I know this is something that old people often say—it made me very sad when the animals got sick or died. I also moved to the country for a while. I started learning about plants and began to grow fond of them. It seemed like a natural transition.

In any case, I guess it must be hereditary or something, but some of my children have grown to be real animal lovers. For their sake, we have started keeping pets again over the last three or four years.

When Naka died, we were making plans to move back to Tokyo the following year. Until we knew whether or not it would be appropriate to have a dog in Tokyo, we decided that we wouldn't get another one, so for a while we didn't keep a dog.

But one day I went for a walk with my children. Following our usual course, we went from the Kasuga Forest to Kasuga Shrine, from the base of Mikasa Mountain to Tamuke Mountain, to Kotsuke Hall and then to the Nigatsu Hall, from Ōgane down the side of Daibutsuden and then around the back to Sashizu Hall at Todaijitatuchū, where I visited the home of my friend Mr. Hashimoto. Right next to the entranceway there was a side door that opened into the garden from which Mrs. Hashimoto emerged followed by three puppies and their mother. The puppies innocently entwined themselves around our feet and wagged their rear ends. As Mr. Hashimoto was out, I decided to return home, but my second youngest daughter, who was crouching down holding a puppy by his neck, did not seem as if she was planning to get up any time soon.

"I want it. I want this dog," she said, looking up at me longingly as if asking for my consent. For some reason, the puppy drooped his tail and remained silent. Though I know it was my imagination, it seemed as if he was worried that he was not going to be adopted. He was a shaggy dog, definitely of mixed breed. Because Mr. Hashimoto was out, I could not ask him if it was all right to take him. But in the end I gave in and decided that if the dog was promised to someone else, we would return him right away, and for the time being, we took the puppy. My children hurried home taking turns holding him.

"We are not taking that dog to Tokyo. When we move back, we're going to have to give him away to someone," I repeatedly reminded the kids. At a time when purebreds like Shepherds, Airedales, and Nihon-kens were in fashion, I did not want to keep this mongrel mutt forever. I also knew something about the wild nature of such dogs and had even written about the subject in a short story entitled "Excursion in the Snow." I had learned from experience about mongrels. He was cute then, but I knew he would not be for long, and I told this to the children.

Two or three days later I received a message from Mr. Hashimoto, saying, "I haven't promised the dog to anyone so you can have him, but you can return him if you think you don't want him." He understood that we had taken the dog because of the children's momentary curiosity and he had the sensitivity to wonder if we were regretting it now. The dog was also of the kind that would inspire such a worry.

The children and I tried to decide on a name for the dog. I had had dogs with names like Teru, Yone, and Toku more than once, and these names were familiar to me. Those dogs each seemed suited to their names, but I felt that they did not suit this dog very well. In the end, weighing the pluses and minuses of several names, since we thought the dog resembled a bear, we decided to call him Kuma.

The following is the opening paragraph of a composition entitled "Kuma" that one of my sons wrote for school:

> Among bears there are brown bears, Japanese bears, white bears, Malaysian bears, but the bear we have in our house is a bear that is not a bear. Kuma is the name of our dog. Kuma is just his name. His fur is clumpy and he looks like a guardian lion as well as a bear, but because he is a dog, he looks like a dog too.

Without a doubt, he is a dog that also looks like a dog.

I often teased K, a boy who lived in our neighborhood, by saying, "We've decided that, when we move to Tokyo, you're going to get Kuma." Whenever I said this, K would force a smile. I also said things like, "It would be so embarrassing if I had to walk this dog in Tokyo from Shimbashi to Kyobashi."

When Kuma was still small, I took him for a walk in Nara Park. A young girl who seemed to be a tourist, stared down at the dog and said "What a strange dog." Kuma had long white and dark brown hair, which didn't grow evenly but in clumps, making him look rather dirty. In front of other people, I always criticized the way Kuma looked, but as time went by, the good points of his personality began to stand out, and I unexpectedly grew fond of him. In my eyes, he became a smart dog with no faults. I realized that this was what it meant to be unable to judge by looks alone.

Once, when the children and I were returning from a rugby match at the Hanazono, we bought two ducks that were about three months old from a Korean. As I carried them in a dirty burlap sack from the back door into the garden, Kuma followed me with extreme curiosity. He could smell the ducks, and his ears were thrust forward and his tail was wagging, upright and stiff.

"Kuma's going to eat the ducks," the children said.

"It's okay. If I'm here he won't." I said. "Hey, Kuma, if you come near here you'll get in big trouble. Understand?"

I tried to tap him lightly on the head, but Kuma dodged my hand, scurrying just out of arm's reach, and moved toward the bag again.

Kuma was part English Setter, so his hunting instincts were strong. If he found a frog in a thicket, he chased it around enthusiastically.

I was a little hesitant, but I let the ducks out of the bag with Kuma present, knowing that if I got angry he would definitely stop. Kuma immediately pounced on them and the garden erupted in a great uproar of the cries of the children, my shouts, and the startled quacking of the ducks. Only Kuma was silent as he chased the ducks. Feathers that had come loose where Kuma nipped at them scattered about. Although they may have seemed slow, the ducks were unexpectedly agile, and in the end they survived without getting bitten.

I caught hold of Kuma and had my sons catch the ducks and bring them to me. I rubbed them in Kuma's nose and spanked him many times. That is how Kuma, now lying on the ground with sad eyes, came to understand that he was not to chase the ducks.

Kuma never bothered the ducks after that. Five or six days later, for some unknown reason, one of the ducks was floating belly up, limp and dead, in the water, in our rectangular, brick-lined pond. Everyone knew that it was not Kuma's fault, and Kuma went unpunished.

Because ducks flock by nature, the one duck that was left got very lonely and began to follow Kuma around the garden. When Kuma lay down, the duck would stretch out and sleep near his nose, burying its head in its own feathers. Kuma did not seem to particularly enjoy this, but the duck, having gotten completely used to Kuma, stuck with him. The duck would follow Kuma even when he went out the garden gate. I knew that this duck that was not afraid of dogs would eventually be killed by one, and sure enough, it was eaten by Taro, our neighbor's dog.

Shortly thereafter, my sons came home with a bunch of chicks, and when they let the chicks go, Kuma, who was sleeping nearby, did not dare come near them. He remembered that he had been scolded for chasing the ducks. Suddenly free, the chicks ran amok. They ran over to where Kuma was sleeping. Because Kuma probably thought that he would get scolded again, he got up with his head drooped. Looking at me out of the corner of his eye, he made an arc around the garden so as not to get close to the chicks and went out the back gate.

The meaning behind Kuma's expression was clear to me. "It's okay now. I'll never do it again, so please don't get angry."

Eventually the chicks also came to trust Kuma and would often climb up on top of him while he was sleeping.

Kuma was indeed a clever dog. The only thing he did that gave us trouble was that, no matter how much we scolded him, he would howl at strangers and sometimes bite them. Because of this, we put him on a long chain during the day and let him loose only at night.

In the fall of the following year, most of my family moved to Tokyo. I stayed behind with my younger daughters who had to finish school. As far as the animals were concerned, our small pet monkey went to Tokyo, and Kuma ended up with us in Nara. When the rest of us moved out the following spring, Kuma came with us.

Although he was smart, Kuma was still a country dog, so we left him chained up for ten days, for fear that he would get himself lost. In the meantime, I took him for walks around the neighborhood and through Toyamagahara. After ten days, I figured Kuma was ready to be let off of the chain, but as I had feared, he disappeared two or three days later. I felt really terrible about it because before he got lost I had gone to Asakusa and had a dog tag made at Nakamise, but I neglected to put it on him and left it hanging on a nail. Had I put it on, we would have still had hope, but unlike in Nara, in Tokyo there was no chance of finding him no matter where we looked.

Even so, I took the kids up to the top of the mountain at the Toyamagahara target range and we called out to Kuma in all directions. It was a bitterly cold, windy evening. I went to the neighborhood police box, but the policeman said he could not go out and look for him. He said that if Kuma did not come back in two or three days, I should file a lost dog report, and once I did that, he would help me look for him.

Getting lost seemed like an uncharacteristic thing for such a clever dog to do. He was a dog that had never even seen a train, so we talked about the possibility that he might have been hit by a Shosen train. Because he was unworldly and often chased cars, we also thought he might have been run over.

Whenever I heard a dog howling in the night, it always sounded like Kuma to me. I would get up, open the window, and call out to him, completely disregarding our neighbors. I also thought of the possibility that after losing his way home, Kuma might have decided to go back to Nara. I remembered a story about a dog from Kishu that was sent to Osaka. After several weeks, the dog found its way back to Kishu, but before it could see its master's face, it dropped dead from exhaustion. I thought that in Kuma's case it would be all the more sad because even if he made it back to Nara, there would be nobody there.

"That could never happen, but just in case, it would be best to send a letter," I said, and had my wife write a letter to the house in Nara. When I imagined Kuma heading west on the Tokaido Highway without any food, I felt terrible.

"How many days has it been?" we wondered.

"Well, he ate dinner on the fourth, so. . . ." We counted the days.

One day I decided to take my son to a bookstore in Kanda to buy workbooks for the children. As we were getting ready to go, a friend of mine stopped by. I had some business with him and it had been a long time since I had seen him. Thinking that I would cancel our trip to Kanda, I spent quite a while with my friend, and then another friend stopped in. By the time my two visitors left, it was after four o'clock.

"What should we do? Should we go? Or should we go tomorrow?" I asked, and my son, laughing sheepishly, said something vague like, "Whichever. We could go today. . . ," which meant that he wanted to go, and it also meant that on the way back he wanted to see a movie or eat a good dinner somewhere.

"You can go buy books later in the evening too. Dinner's almost ready so why don't you go after you eat?" my eldest daughter said, teasing my son just to be spiteful.

"Shut up. Don't butt in," he responded.

My son, upset because she had seen through him, glared at his sister.

We decided to go after all, and I took my son and his younger sister and left. When we tried to get on the city bus that runs from Takadanobaba to Tokyo Station, it was so full of passengers that we would have had to stand, so we decided to wait for the next one. When the next bus came, my son rushed on first to save us seats. It was a tight squeeze, but we were able to sit together.

When the bus passed the intersection at Edogawa Bridge, by chance I looked outside and saw a dog trotting across the bridge toward Gokoku Temple. From a distance, it looked like Kuma. The upright tail looked a little different, and I wondered if I was just wishing it looked like Kuma, but when I asked the kids, "Isn't that Kuma?" Tazuko, my daughter who loves animals the most of any of us, stood up and said in an excited voice, "It's Kuma! It's Kuma!"

The bus had already crossed the intersection, and my view of the dog was blocked by a house, so I could not see him anymore. I said to my children, "Wait for me at the next stop," and got up, but the bus attendant stopped me and said, "Please wait for the next stop."

"I see our lost dog. Please let me off," I said.

"Rules are rules," she said.

I pushed the woman aside. The bus driver, without a word, slowed down so that I could get off.

When I got to the bridge, the dog (I did not know yet whether or not it was Kuma) was running at the same pace as me, more than a block away.

I called out in a loud voice, "Kuma! Kuma!" but the dog did not even look back. The only way to catch up with him was to run faster. I tried running as fast as I could, but it was not fast enough. I had thought of myself as a strong runner, but in reality, it was just a memory from the past. My present body completely disregarded what I told it to do. I was thankful that I was not wearing Japanese-style clothes, but my coat still felt heavy and I gradually became tired. As I chased Kuma, I confirmed that it was in fact him, but no matter how loudly I called to him, he did not hear me. Thinking that if I lost sight of him then I might never see him again, I unabashedly cried,"Kuma! Kuma!"

To make matters worse, not one taxi went by as I was running. I felt as if I were going to pass out. I could not keep up anymore and it pained me to see the distance between myself and Kuma grow gradually larger.

Then, another dog came from the opposite direction and Kuma stopped. They sniffed each other a little and I thought if they would only get into a fight I would be able to chase Kuma down, but the dogs separated immediately and Kuma continued running away, resuming his pace.

I saw a parked car on the opposite side of the street so I hurried across, only to find a little girl about four years old sitting in the driver's seat. I did not see the driver anywhere.

"Is it that dog?" asked a young factory worker wearing a military-style hat. He got on the bicycle he had at his side and chased Kuma for me. The young man must have seen me chasing Kuma, since I had not said anything to him. I felt exhausted, as if I had used up all of the strength in my body. I wiped the sweat from my forehead as I walked, wondering if he would be able to catch Kuma and if Kuma would bite him. The young man soon caught up with

Kuma, but perhaps because he was scared of him, he did not try to take hold of him, and instead I saw that he was just following him on his bicycle.

An empty taxi came by so I hailed it.

"It's a big brown dog, right?" the driver said. It was good luck that he had come from the opposite direction and had seen Kuma.

I was finally able to catch Kuma at the gate of Gokoku Temple. I tried to give the youth with the bicycle a tip. He would not take it, so I had to force it on him. I returned with Kuma in the taxi to pick up my kids who were waiting at Edogawa Bridge. We decided not to go to Kanda and returned straight home.

When I tell people this story, they often say, "Kuma must have been very happy to see you," but the truth is, at that time, Kuma did not seem as happy as I expected him to be. It might have been because Kuma was exhausted. If he had been any more tired, he might have just keeled over like that dog from Kishu. I think he might also have been a little dazed from his daily hardships. But, when we arrived at Edogawa Bridge and my son and daughter got in the taxi, it seemed as though Kuma finally realized that he had been saved and he became very happy. He put his front paws on both my shoulders and no matter how many times I removed them, trying to make him sit, Kuma kept putting his paws back on my shoulders and panted. He stayed thay way until we got home.

Kuma had been gone for a week.

As we had all but given up hope of ever finding him, everyone at home was extremely happy to see Kuma. We immediately put him on the chain and gave him milk and buttered bread. One of the kids even gave him a cream puff. At first Kuma gobbled it all up, but after a while, he hung his head between his extended paws and opened and closed his already half-shut eyes, as if to say he wanted to sleep.

"Maybe it was just a coincidence, but I feel like it was more than that," I said.

"We're so lucky. He's home to stay," said my wife.

"What should we do about the Airedale we ordered from Mr. Tanaka? Should we cancel it?" I asked.

"I guess so. If we had two dogs, I'd feel guilty for not paying enough attention to Kuma. I guess we should cancel it," she said.

"I doubt that would happen, but we should cancel it anyway. Please call him right away," I said.

The more I thought about it, the more mysterious it seemed. That day I had guests, so I couldn't leave home until late, and the bus was crowded so we skipped one, and on top of all that, if we had been sitting facing the other way on the bus, we would never have seen Kuma. When the bus was crossing the intersection he happened to be right outside the window. Everything really worked out well. I guess things sometimes just work out, but even so, I do not know if you can just simply say that it was chance.

For two or three days I limped around with aching calves. Kuma was completely wiped out too and all he did was sleep, but before long he became the same lively Kuma that he had been before. And the strange thing is that after all this happened, Kuma became more obedient with me. He is always kind toward members of our own family, but it is still a different story when it comes to strangers.

NEWS OF THE EARTHQUAKE

Nakano Shigeharu

There was a big earthquake in Fukui Prefecture on the evening of June 28, 1948 (the twenty-third year of the reign of the Showa Emperor). The news was in the Tokyo newspaper on the twenty-ninth. The paper said that the core of the earthquake was toward the end of the Kuzuryū River that runs through Fukui.

"It must have been in the Sakai District," I thought.

I knew this because I was born in Fukui Prefecture. I know the Kuzuryū River well. I swam in that river when I was a child. Unlike in Tokyo, the water is blue and there are fish swimming in it.

Two days later, I found out that the core of the earthquake, the epicenter, was in fact not at the mouth of the Kuzuryū River, but somewhere between the village of East Jūgō and the town of Maruoka. It was then that I prepared myself for the worst. I did so by telling myself, "My house has been flattened like a pancake."

The village of Takaboko is between the village of East Jūgō and the town of Maruoka. My house was in Takaboko. It was an old, old house, and there was no doubt in my mind that the house had been destroyed by the earthquake.

I received a telegram from home.

"HOUSE DESTROYED. EVERYONE FINE," it read.

The house had been destroyed. I wondered how my sick mother, who was seventy-six years old, had been able to escape. I felt I had to go there, no matter what.

So I went to Fukui Prefecture, to my destroyed house, and I went to nearby villages and towns and looked around and got to thinking. I would like to share some of the thoughts I had then with you.

They said that cars and trucks could not pass because the ground had split and there were cracks in the roads. Although I am not a child, at first I did not understand why. Even if there were cracks in the road, a truck's tires could surely get over them, I thought.

But when I saw the road I quickly understood why. Cracks ran down the middle of every single road. If the cracks had formed across the road, you would have been able to get across them, but because they ran down the middle of the road, a truck's tires would have fallen right in, so there was no way they could get down the road.

If the road were three meters wide and the cracks ran down the middle of the road, then between the cracks, there was only a very narrow piece of the road left. To be more exact, if there was a road that was three meters wide and there were two cracks running down it, the road was split into three sections that were one meter wide each. There were at least two or three cracks running down each road, so wide roads that were three or five meters wide were divided into many narrow paths. And the cracks were very deep, up to a meter deep. That was why trucks could not get over them, and cars could not get down the road. How the roads crack in a big earthquake is one of the things I wanted to tell you about.

When I went to my village, not one house was left standing. People had leaned boards against trees and were living in temporary shelters. And because they were hastily made, if the wind blew, the roof would fall down. If it rained, water would leak through. It was urgent that we build a real house right away.

But before we could build a real house, we had to break down the old house and clear away the rubble. This is a very difficult thing to do. In the first place, farmers' houses, unlike houses in towns, are built to be very strong. They are built using wide logs. So if a house like this falls down, it is much harder to clear away than a regular house. Not just anyone can do this. You have to have a carpenter do it. Or if not a carpenter, then you have to get someone whose specialty it is to do it. There are specialists like this in every village.

However, it was difficult to get specialists to come to our house because their own houses had also been destroyed. Every carpenter's house had been destroyed. Every house as far as you could see had been destroyed. From the point of view of the carpenter, it was most important to fix his own house first. If he did not do this, he would not be able to go elsewhere to work. That is why we couldn't get them to come so easily. We all usually think that we can look after ourselves, but I came to realize then that this is not true. To build one house, you need the lumberjack who cuts down the trees; the mill worker who cuts the logs into boards and beams; the people who carry the wood on cars, trains, and boats; the person who designs the house; the carpenters who build the house; the women who make food to feed the carpenters; as well as many others. Only after you combine the efforts of all these

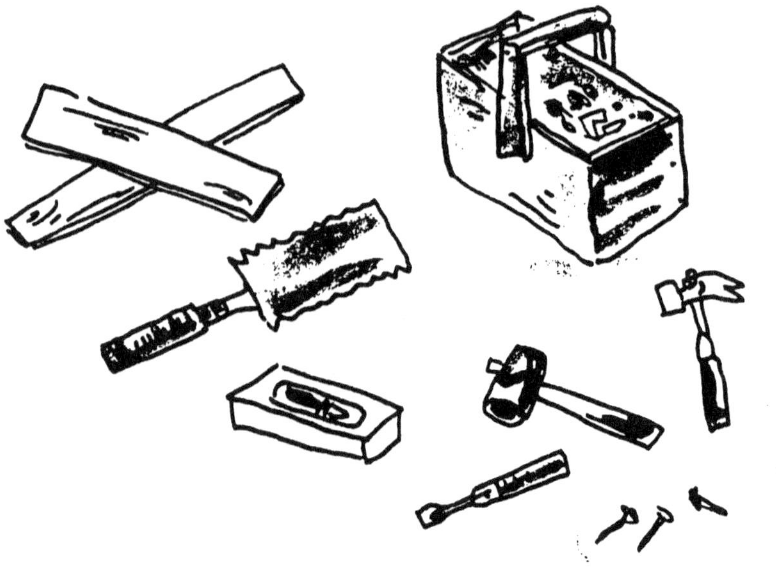

people can a house be built. I came to understand this well after the earthquake. That was the second thing I wanted to tell you.

So, as I waited for the work to begin, I began to think about people from long ago. When I say people from long ago, I do not mean a hundred or two hundred years ago. I mean people from a thousand or two thousand years ago.

We tend to think that these people from the past were uncivilized. These people did not have electricity. They had no trains. They of course had no newspapers or glass. If they went somewhere, they would walk there on their own feet. They built their homes themselves. And in order to build a home, they would cut down trees themselves. They would lay the foundation themselves. And they would construct it themselves. And they would paint the walls themselves, and so on. One person might be a farmer, a fisherman, a carpenter, a weather forecaster, a bridge builder, and a well digger, all at the same time.

Of course, it's not that simple. Even those people from long ago had division of labor. If someone were going to build a house back then, there is no doubt that a lot of other people helped out. Even so, the people from that time could not just say that if their gas was turned off, they could not make dinner; or if people were hurt, they couldn't just go to a hospital. In other words, they all had to be doctors. Therefore, even though those people from long ago were not civilized, they were wise. They knew a lot about many different things. And they were people who were able to do a lot of different things. They were not civilized people, but they were smarter than we who are civilized, and they were people who could do a wide variety of things. Although we are living in an era of conveniences, we really need to become people who can take care of ourselves by ourselves.

This is the third thing I wanted to tell you.

THE STONEMILL'S SONG

Tsuboi Sakae

1

Out in the country, August is the month of the *obon* festival, when people celebrate the spirits of their ancestors. It is a tradition to make dumplings and noodles during the obon season by grinding wheat, rice, and roasted soybeans into flour. That is why, once August begins, here and there, in every home, you can hear the grinding songs of the stonemill.

Chieko now loved the stonemill's songs, but before she came to love them, she had really hated them because she found the grinding sound so boring that it made her sleepy.

It was usually Chieko's grandmother who would work the stonemill, but when she had to grind wheat or raw soybeans, the work would get very hard, so she would have Chieko help her. When Chieko sat across from her grandmother to turn the mill, at first it would make a quick, energetic sound, but soon the sound would begin to slow down until all she heard was a low rumble. This is because Chieko would soon grow drowsy either from the hard work or from boredom. If Chieko seemed bored, her grandmother would begin to tell her stories from long ago, but at these times Chieko did not find the stories the least bit interesting. What's more, they were all stories she had already heard before.

"You told me that one already," she would say, letting out a sigh. Chieko's grandmother told stories about the time her own grandfather, when he was still a young man, had to cut off his topknot because of a new law that was passed banning long hair,

or about how when she herself was first married, wild boars from the mountains would cause her much grief when they came down to the village and wrecked her garden, or about how as a young girl she was once out drying the laundry when a wild boar that was being chased by hunters ran past her and got away.

During the winter when she was sitting near the fire warming herself, Chieko found these stories interesting no matter how many times she heard them, but when she was turning the mill, she did not find them interesting at all.

Seeing that Chieko was bored, her grandmother would smile and begin to turn the mill faster. "Listen Chieko, the mill is singing, '*If you want dumplings, turn the mill! If you want dumplings, turn the mill!*'"

Chieko would listen carefully, and the mill, which until then seemed to be making a sleepy noise, really sounded as if it were singing, "'*If you want dumplings, turn the mill*!'" like her grandmother said. Chieko would let out a laugh and sing along. "'*If you want dumplings, turn the mill! If you want dumplings, turn the mill!*'" Then the mill would suddenly become light and her sleepiness would disappear.

Chieko once tried singing, "'*I don't want any dumplings so I'm not going to turn the mill!*'" But this song did not match the rhythm of the mill at all.

"You can't lie to the mill. Your face gives it away. '*You want dumplings, so let's turn the mill!*'" her grandmother sang as she turned the mill. And the mill sang along with her.

The mill will only sing about the true feelings of the person who is turning it. "Just now, the mill saw your tired face and was singing, '*I'm sleepy! I'm sleepy!*' It only continued to turn because I'm not tired. If you were turning it alone, both you and the mill would have fallen asleep by now," Chieko's grandmother said.

2

During obon season, there was something else that Chieko looked forward to. Her cousin Mizue, who lived in Hiroshima, used to come for a visit. Every year, two or three people from Mizue's family would come at the beginning of the new year and during obon to pay their respects at the family gravesite. Because of the war, however, no one had come in recent years. As the war continued, people who lived in the cities could no longer safely send their children to school. Thus, it was decided that Mizue was to be evacuated to the country to live with her grandmother. Mizue's father was Chieko's father's younger brother, so they both had the same grandmother.

"When our relatives from Hiroshima come, we'll feed them lots of dumplings. They'll be so happy, because children in the city get only get rations," Chieko's grandmother said.

Then Chieko's mother added, "Even if we have no sugar, let's make candy and sweet drinks."

Chieko chimed in, "And I'll give Mizue half of my sugar cane!"

This was the first year they had tried to grow sugar cane in the corner of their garden, and Chieko had decided that all of it belonged to her. The sugar cane had already grown big, thick leaves.

"I hope Mizue comes soon. If she doesn't come soon, the corn will get too ripe," Chieko said.

They had received a letter from their relatives saying that they would arrive at the beginning of August, but it was already the third and they had not come. For the third day in a row, Chieko wandered out to the docks around the time the boats came in.

"They'll definitely be there today," she thought.

She wondered how big Mizue had gotten. Mizue was in the third grade, so she was probably as tall as Kiku, their neighbor.

"I'll treat her like a younger sister. And every day I'll take her with me to school. And I'll share my garden with her and in the fall we can plant crops. Mizue is from the city so she's probably not very good at planting. Together we will grow cabbages like the one I won second prize for in the farming contest. If we grow a good one, I'm going to give it to her," she thought.

Chieko walked along deaming happy daydreams. The steamship had already come into the harbor and she could hear people's voices on the deck. The passengers had the afternoon sun to their backs so Chieko could not see them clearly. She put up her right hand to block the sun, trying to find Mizue in the large crowd of faces.

"Chie!" someone called from the boat.

"Yes!" Chieko replied. No matter how much she squinted, she could not see who it was. But she was sure that she had heard her aunt's voice calling out to her. Chieko knitted her brows and shielded her eyes with both hands.

"We're over here, Chie!" she heard Mizue call out as she clapped her hands. When Chieko finally saw Mizue, she was already coming down the ramp onto the pier wearing a dark, striped jacket and patterned pants. She also had a patterned air raid cap slung over her shoulder and was carrying a small bag. She was followed by Chieko's aunt.

"Welcome! This is the third day I've come out to meet the boat," Chieko said.

The three of them walked side by side. Although Mizue was three years younger, she was almost the same height as Chieko.

"Chie, please look after Mizue like a younger sister," Chieko's aunt said as she walked. And then she said to Mizue, "And you treat Chie like an older sister."

Chieko was embarassed and looked down at the ground. She was embarassed because, as the youngest child in her family, she had never been treated like an older sister by anyone, but from that day she was to be Mizue's older sister. But it also made her very happy and she even felt that she had grown a little bigger.

When they got to the house, Chieko's mother and grandmother began chatting with Chieko's aunt. Cheiko sat down next to her grandmother's mill and began turning it by herself. The mill sang out, "'*You're a big sister! You're a big sister!*' "

By then, they had ground a lot of flour to make dumplings. They had decided to grind some extra to give to Chieko's aunt as a present. As they were putting the different kinds of flour into separate bags, Chieko's aunt said politely, "I can't accept all this flour that you worked so hard to grind"

Hearing this, Chieko said, "Don't worry. We all help to grind the flour, and from now on Mizue will help out too so we'll be able to make lots more. It's fun!"

"But it must be very tiring," Chieko's aunt said.

"When I get tired, I sing. '*If you want dumplings, turn the mill!*' Then the mill gets very light," Chieko said.

Everyone found this funny and they all laughed a lot. Even after everyone else had stopped laughing, Chieko's aunt continued to laugh.

3

After staying for two nights, Chieko's aunt went back to Hiroshima, before the start of the obon festival. On the evening of her departure, she, Chieko, and Mizue went to visit their family gravesite. As they stood at the graveyard on the top of the hill looking out over the village Chieko's aunt said, "No matter how many times I look at this view, I never get tired of it. You are very lucky, Mizue, to be able to live in a place like this. Some day, your father and I will rest here with our ancestors. It's a wonderful place."

"It's a wonderful place," she repeated.

Then, as an offering, they placed flowers and water at each grave. How could they have known then that Chieko's aunt's words would come back to haunt them only four or five days later?

Chieko's aunt must have returned to her house in Hiroshima in the early morning on August 6. As soon as she got back, she must have started to prepare breakfast for everyone in the house. Forgetting her tiredness, she spoke about Chieko and Mizue with everyone. Then she probably took out the dried fish and flour she received as a gift and told everyone about the stonemill's song and everyone probably had a good laugh. Chieko's uncle and everyone else in the house must have really enjoyed hearing all the stories about life in the country.

This is the way they imagined it.

"Right about now my mom is probably making bread, because my father loves bread. He probably said to her, 'Hey, make me a loaf!'" Mizue said, remembering her home fondly. Everyone thought it was so funny the way she mimicked her father, and they all laughed. Mizue was so excited because everything was new to her—eating breakfast on a bench in the garden, the plum blossoms painted on her bowl, the yard with the persimon and chestnut trees in full bloom. The obon festival was about to begin. Mizue was told that on the morning of the obon festival, before the sun comes up, all the people in the village put on their best kimonos and go to visit their ancestors' graves. She also heard that, in the main building of the temple, they bring out the treasured six-paneled screen

with scenes from heaven and hell painted on them for all to see. Mizue found every single thing she was told new and interesting.

Mizue passed the morning of August 6, the first morning that she spent in the country away from her family, learning many wonderful things. Who could have imagined that, on that morning, her house in Hiroshima would be burned to the ground and her father and mother would be nowhere to be found?

It was a clear morning. One would suppose that, like Mizue, her father and mother started that clear day without a care. But in fact her father and mother were already gone.

Mizue looked as if she might cry at any moment. Chieko tried her hardest to console her. "The two of us will study hard together," Chieko said. Mizue nodded in silence.

The next day was already the thirteenth, the day of the obon festival. They were to clean their ancestors' gravestones and make an offering to the dead, but the mill remained still. It seemed to be crying next to Chieko's grandmother, who sat silent, deep in thought.

"I'll turn the mill," Chieko said sweetly, hoping to console her grandmother. She sat down next to the mill.

"My grandmother is so weak. She has no strength left," Chieko thought as she grasped the handle of the mill and began turning. To make dumplings for the offering, you have to make rice flour, so the mill was very hard to turn.

"Chieko, I'll help you," Mizue said, and she took hold of the handle. Mizue was not yet used to turning the mill, but with the two of them working together, it was half as heavy. Seeing the two girls working together made Chieko's grandmother sniffle. Chieko pretended not to notice this and turned the mill quickly.

"'*Work hard! Work hard! Endure the unendurable. . . !*'" The mill began to sing as beads of sweat formed on Chieko and Mizue's faces.

THE SNOWY NIGHT

Dazai Osamu

That day, it had been snowing since morning. The pants I had sewn for Tsuru were finished, so I stopped at my aunt's house in Nakano to deliver them on the way home from school. When I left, she gave me two sheets of dried squid as a present.

By the time I reached Kichijōji Station, it had already gotten dark and there was over a foot of snow on the ground and the snow continued to fall without stopping. I was wearing boots and was excited to see all the snow, so I purposely walked where it was deepest. As I reached the mailbox near my house, I realized that I no longer had the dried squid wrapped in newspaper under my arm. I tend to be absent-minded sometimes, but I don't usually lose things. That night, however, perhaps because I was excited by the snow, I had dropped my package. I was distraught.

Now, to get upset about dropping some dried squid is rather silly and I'm embarrassed to admit it, but I was planning on giving the squid to Kimiko, my brother's wife, who lives with us. She is going to have a baby this summer. She said that when you have a baby in your belly, you get really hungry. You have to eat enough for the baby too, so it's like eating for two. Unlike me, Kimiko pays great attention to her personal appearance and is an elegant woman. Until recently, she ate like a bird and never snacked, but lately she says she's embarrassingly hungry and she craves odd things.

I had not forgotten that a few days earlier, as Kimiko and I were cleaning up after dinner, she said she had a really bitter taste in her mouth. She sighed and said quietly that she would like to snack on

some dried squid, and just by chance that day I received two sheets of dried squid from my aunt, so I planned to give it to Kimiko as a surprise, but I lost it. That's why I was so upset.

As you know, my older brother, his wife Kimiko, and I live in our house together. My brother is an eccentric writer who is now almost forty and is not even a little famous. He is always poor, often says that he is unwell, and always stays at home. He talks a lot and complains all the time and doesn't help out around the house at all, so poor Kimiko has to do everything.

One day, when I was feeling especially angry at my brother I said to him, "Do you think every once in a while you could take the shopping bag and go to buy some vegetables? Other husbands do that, I hear."

He got really mad at me and said, "You're so stupid! I'm not a common man. Do you understand? Kimiko, you listen carefully too. Even if we were starving to death I wouldn't disgrace myself by going shopping, so why don't you just accept it? And that's my final word."

Well that's all fine and good, but in my brother's case, I'm not sure whether he is refusing to go shopping for the good of the country or out of laziness.

My father and mother both came from Tokyo, but my father worked for a government office in Tohoku for a long time and both my brother and I were born up north in Yamagata. My father died there, and when my brother was around twenty and I was still just a small child, my mother put me on her back and the three of us came to Tokyo. Last year my mother also died and now its just my brother and his wife and myself in the house. We don't really have any other family, so it's not as if we can have food sent in from our relatives in the country like other families. Since my brother is such a strange person, we seldom entertain guests, so I rarely get my hands on anything out of the ordinary. Therefore if I had given my sister those two sheets of dried squid it would have made her very happy—so even though it seems silly, I had really treasured those two sheets of dried squid. I turned right around and went back down that snowy street to look for them.

But there was no way I was going to find them. Besides the fact that it is very difficult to find something wrapped in white newspaper on a white snowy street, the snow had continued to fall, so on my way back to the station, all I could see was new snow on the ground. I sighed and adjusted my umbrella, and as I looked up into the dark night sky I saw the snow falling like millions of fireflies dancing around in a frenzy. How beautiful it was, I thought. The trees on both sides of the street were covered with snow and the branches were sagging from the weight, and every once in a while, as if they were sighing, they would stir slightly. Lost in this fairy-tale world, I had completely forgotten about the dried squid.

Just then I had a great idea. I would bring this beautiful snowy night to Kimiko as a present. It was a much better present than dried squid. I was very embarassed that I had been so silly as to get carried away about some stupid squid.

My brother once told me that people's eyes can store what they see. The proof is that when you glance at a light bulb and then close your eyes you can still see an image of the light bulb on the underside of your eyelids. My brother also once told me a story about something that happened long ago in Denmark, and even though my brother's stories are always nonsense and they are never true, I really wanted to believe this one. Even if he had made it up and none of it were true, I thought it was a pretty good story.

Long ago a doctor in Denmark was doing an autopsy on a young sailor who had died in a shipwreck. When the doctor looked at the sailor's eye under a microscope, he saw an image of a happy family imprinted on his retina. The doctor told a writer friend of his about the eye and the writer came up with the following explanation of this mysterious image.

The young sailor had fallen into the sea and was swallowed up by a big wave and was thrown against a cliff and in his struggle to save himself he grabbed onto the windowsill of a lighthouse. The sailor was very happy that he was going to be saved, but when he looked through the window he saw a family about to begin eating a modest but happy dinner, and he thought to himself, 'I can't cry out for help right now because that would ruin this happy family scene.' At that moment, the sailor lost his grip on the windowsill and a huge wave came and dragged him out into the open sea. The writer was sure that this is what had happened, and that this sailor was the most kind and noble person in the world. The doctor believed this story and the two of them respectfully buried the body of the sailor. This was the story my brother told me.

I want to believe this story is true. Even if it cannot be proved scientifically, I want to believe it. I thought of the story on that snowy night, and I planned to save the beautiful image of the snowy land-

scape in the depths of my eyes and go home and say to Kimiko, "Look into my eyes, and the baby in your stomach will be beautiful!"

Just recently, Kimiko asked my brother to put pictures of beautiful people on the walls of her room. She thought that if she looked at them every day she would have a beautiful child. My brother took her very seriously and said, "Hmm. Prenatal care. Very important." He put up two pictures next to each other on the wall, one of an elegant Noh mask called Magojirō and one of a cute Noh mask called Yuki No Ko Omote, which was very good of him to do, but then he went on to put up a picture of himself making an awful face right between the two Noh masks, which canceled out the two nice pictures completely.

"I beg you, please take down the picture of yourself. When I look at it I begin to feel sick." Kimiko, who is usually very quiet, probably could not stand it any longer, and pleaded with my brother, and in the end he allowed the picture of himself to be taken down. I know that if Kimiko had to look at the picture of my brother any longer she would give birth to a monkey-faced baby. My brother is rather strange looking, but I think he sees himself as handsome. He's hopeless.

For the sake of the baby in her stomach, Kimiko only wants to look at the most beautiful things in the world. I knew that if I recorded the sight of the snowy landscape in the depths of my eyes and showed it to her she would be a hundred times happier than if she had received a gift of dried squid. So, I gave up on trying to find the dried squid and on the way back home I did my best to take in the beautiful snowy landscape. I arrived home feeling filled, not only in the depths of my eyes, but deep in my heart, with the pure whiteness of the beautiful landscape.

As soon as I got home I said to my sister, "Look into my eyes. In the depths of my eyes there is a beautiful landscape."

"What? What are you talking about?" she asked, laughing as she put her hand on my shoulder. "What happened to your eyes?"

"It's like the story my brother once told us. A person can capture something they see in the depths of their eyes."

"What story? I forgot that story. His stories usually aren't true anyway," she said.

"But that story was true. Just that one. Look into my eyes. I just looked at all the beautiful snow outside. If you look into my eyes, you will give birth to a beautiful baby with skin like snow."

With a sad expression on her face, Kimiko silently looked into my eyes.

"Hey!"

Just then my brother came into the room. "Don't look into those useless eyes. It would be a hundred times better to look into my eyes," he said.

"Why? Why?" I asked. I was so mad at my brother I wanted to hit him. "Kimiko said that when she looks into your eyes she gets sick to her stomach."

"That can't be true. My eyes have gazed upon beautiful snowy landscapes for twenty years. I lived in Yamagata until I was around twenty. You came to Tokyo before you could really know the beautiful landscapes of Yamagata. It's silly to be making such a big deal out of this second-rate Tokyo landscape. My eyes have seen a hundred, a thousand, infinitely more beautiful snowy landscapes than yours, so no matter what you say, my eyes are better than yours."

I was so upset I thought I was going to cry. But Kimiko came to my rescue. With a smile, she said to my brother in a quiet voice, "It may be true that you've seen a hundred or a thousand times more beautiful things, but then it is also true that you've seen twice as many, a thousand times as many ugly things."

"Yeah, that's right. The minuses outweigh the pluses. That's why your eyes are so yellow. Ha!" I said to him.

"How dare you speak to me like that!" my brother said, and left the room.

THE SPIDER'S THREAD

Akutagawa Ryūnosuke

1

One day Buddha was strolling alone around the edge of the lotus pond in paradise. The lotus flowers growing in the pond were as white as pearls, and their yellow centers continuously overflowed with an indescribably pleasant fragrance. It was morning in paradise.

Buddha stood at the edge of the pond and looked between the lotus leaves on the surface of the water to see what was going on below. As the depths of hell were directly below the lotus pond in paradise, the River Styx and the Mountain of Needles were in such sharp focus through the crystal clear water it was as if one were looking through a spyglass.

Buddha's gaze fell upon a man named Kandata, who was writhing in the depths of hell along with all of the other sinners. Kandata was an infamous thief who had killed people, burnt down houses, and done many other evil deeds, but he had also done one good thing during his life. One day Kandata was walking through the forest when he saw a small spider crawling along the side of the road. Just when he was about to step on the spider to kill it, he suddenly thought to himself, "No, no. Even though this spider is small, it is still a living creature. It would be wrong to take its life for no reason," and he spared the spider's life.

As Buddha was looking down into hell, he remembered that Kandata had once saved a spider's life. And to repay this one good deed, he thought he would try to rescue Kandata. Happily,

as he looked around, he saw a spider of paradise sitting on a jade-colored lotus leaf spinning a beautiful silvery thread. Buddha carefully took the thread in his hand and lowered it between the pearly white lotus flowers into the depths of hell.

2

Kandata was rising and sinking in the Lake of Blood along with the other sinners in the depths of hell. It was pitch dark, and, looking down, all one could see was the occasional glint of a needle on the frightening Mountain of Needles. It was indescribably bleak. It was also as silent as a graveyard, except for the occasional faint meaning of the sinners. The sinners had already undergone the tortures of hell and did not even have the strength to scream. Kandata, the infamous thief, could only flounder like a dying frog as he choked on the blood from the Lake of Blood.

For a moment, Kandata happened to look up at the sky above the Lake of Blood and in the silent darkness from the far-away sky he saw a glistening silvery spider's thread—so thin and delicate it seemed afraid to be seen—descending over his head. When he saw this, Kandata's hands clapped with joy. He had no doubt that if he climbed up this thread he would be able to get himself out of hell. If things went well, he might even make it up to paradise. He would then no longer be chased up the Mountain of Needles, nor would he be drowned in the Lake of Blood.

With this in mind, Kandata gripped the the spider's thread tightly with both hands and began pulling himself upward with all his might. He had been an infamous thief so he was accustomed to doing such things.

The distance between hell and paradise, however, is great, and no matter how much Kandata struggled, he could not easily climb to the top. Finally Kandata became so tired that he could not climb any higher. He had no choice but to take a rest, and as he hung from the thread, he looked down far below him.

From this height, which he had reached with such great effort, the Lake of Blood, in which he had been submerged until so recently, had disappeared into the darkness. The faint glimmer of the Mountain of Needles was also well below him. If he continued at this rate, it would be easier than he had thought to get out of hell. Gripping the spider's thread with both hands Kandata yelled out in a voice he hadn't used in many years, "I made it! I made it!"

Just then he noticed that a countless number of sinners were desperately climbing up the spider's thread after him like a procession of ants. When he saw this, Kandata was struck by a combination of surprise and terror, so for a while all he could do was

watch with his mouth wide open. He wondered how the thin spider's thread, which seemed as if it would break under just his own weight, could hold the weight of so many people. If by chance the thread broke, he, after having made such efforts to climb to this point, would fall head first back into hell. It would be terrible if such a thing happened.

Meanwhile, the hundreds or even thousands of sinners continued to crawl up the thin glimmering spider's thread single file, from the bottom of the dark Lake of Blood. He had to do something before the thread broke in two and he fell.

Kandata yelled out, "Hey, you sinners. This is my spider's thread. Who gave you permission to climb it? Get off. Get off."

Suddenly the spider's thread, which had shown no signs of breaking until then, snapped where Kandata had been hanging. Kandata was helpless. In an instant, he plunged downward, spinning like a top as he fell head over heels into the depths of darkness.

In the end, all that remained was a short piece of the wispy spider's thread of paradise glimmering in the moonless, starless sky.

3

Buddha had been standing at the edge of the lotus pond watching these events from beginning to end, and when he saw Kandata fall like a stone into the bottom of the Lake of Blood, his expression became sad as he resumed his stroll. From Buddha's viewpoint, it was most pitiful that Kandata's merciless heart made him try to save only himself, and he was punished by being returned to hell.

But the lotus flowers on the pond in paradise paid no attention to such things. The pearly white flowers rustled their petals around Buddha's feet, and their yellow centers continuously overflowed with the most indescribably pleasant fragrance. It was nearing noon in paradise.

GON THE FOX

Niimi Nankichi

1

This is a story I heard from an old man in my village named Mohei when I was very young.

Long ago, in nearby Nakayama, there was a small castle where a lord named Nakayama used to live. And in the mountains just a short distance from Nakayama lived a fox named Gon. He was a young fox who lived all alone in a nest he had dug among the thick ferns in the forest. Day and night, he would come out into the surrounding villages and cause trouble.

He would go into the fields and dig up potatoes and throw them all over the place, he would set fire to seeds left out to dry, and he would go into the farmers' backyards and rip down all the hot peppers they had strung up. He did all kinds of mischievous things.

One autumn it rained for two or three days straight. Gon could not go outside and had to stay crouched in his nest. When the rain stopped, Gon was relieved and crawled out of his nest. The sky was very clear and the birds were singing.

Gon went down to the bank of the river. The grass was sprinkled with glistening raindrops. The river was usually quite low, but because it had rained for so long, it had gotten rather high. All the plants, which were usually on dry land, were being tossed to and fro by the swollen river.

Gon trotted downstream along a muddy path. By chance he looked over and saw someone standing in the river. In order not to be seen, Gon crept closer through the high grass.

"It's Hyōju," thought Gon. Hyōju had his tattered black kimono pulled up and stood in waist-high water shaking the big fishing net he had strung up across the river. He was wearing a headband, and there was a round clover leaf stuck like a big mole to the side of his face.

After a while, Hyōju pulled a small bag that was attached to his net out of the water. Inside the bag were roots and grass and rotten twigs, and also some things that were white and shiny. They were fat eels and big fish. Hyōju pulled the eels and fish, along with everything else, out of the bag and stuffed it all into his basket. He put the bag back into the water, got out of the river and placed the basket on the bank, and then, as if he were looking for something, went running upriver.

When Hyōju was out of sight, Gon dashed out from the tall grass and ran to the basket. He was feeling mischievous. Gon pulled the fish out of the basket and, aiming downriver from the net, began tossing them into the water one by one. Each fish made a big splash in the muddy water and then swam away. Gon tried to grab the fat eel, but it was so slimy that he couldn't hold onto it. Gon became impatient and stuck his head in the bag, taking hold of the eel's head with his teeth. The eel let out a shriek and wrapped itself around Gon's neck.

Just then, Hyōju yelled from downstream, "Hey, that fox is a thief!"

Gon was startled and jumped up. He tried to pry the eel off his neck and run away but the eel stayed wrapped around him and wouldn't come loose.

With the eel still clinging to his neck, Gon stumbled away. He stopped beneath a tree near his nest and looked back, but Hyōju was not running after him. Gon sighed with relief and then freed himself from the eel by biting off its head, leaving it on the grass outside his nest.

2

Ten days later, as Gon ran through the back yard of Yasuke the farmer, he saw Yasuke's wife grooming herself in the shade of a fig tree. And as he passed through the back of Shinbē the blacksmith's house, he noticed Shinbē's wife brushing her hair.

"There's something going on in the village," Gon thought. "I wonder what it is. Is it the Autumn Festival? If it were a festival, then you would be able to hear drums and flutes. And there would be banners up at the shrine."

Gon walked along, trying to figure out what was going on, and before he knew it he came to the red well in front of Hyōju's house. There was a large crowd of people inside his shabby home. A group of women who were all dressed up were stoking the flame of an outdoor stove. There was something cooking in a big pot.

"Aha! It's a funeral," thought Gon. "Someone in Hyōju's family must have died."

That afternoon, Gon went over to the village cemetery and hid behind a statue. It was a fine day, and the roof tiles of the castle sparkled in the distance. A patch of red flowers wove themselves together like a piece of thick cloth. The sound of a bell ringing floated up from the village. This signaled the coming of the funeral procession. Gon caught glimpses of people dressed in white kimonos approaching. Their voices grew louder as the procession entered the cemetery. After the procession had passed, the red flowers lay bent and broken.

Gon stood on his toes and watched. Hyōju was wearing a ceremonial jacket and carrying a Buddhist tablet. His face, which usually looked as healthy as a rosy potato, seemed somehow wilted today.

"It was Hyōju's mother who died," Gon thought, pulling his head into his shoulders.

That night, Gon sat in his nest thinking. "I bet that Hyōju's mother, who was probably sick in bed, had said that she wanted to eat eel. And so Hyōju went out with his fishing net to catch eel. But I wanted to cause trouble so I took the eel. And so Hyōju wasn't able to give his mother the eel. And then she died. She died thinking, 'I want to eat some eel, I want to eat some eel!' If I had just left Hyōju alone, everything would be okay."

3

Hyōju stood washing barley at his red well. He and his mother had lived together in poverty. But now that his mother was dead, Hyōju was all alone.

"Hyōju is all alone just like me," Gon thought, as he watched from behind the storeroom. Just as Gon turned to leave, he heard the voice of the sardine salesman.

"Sardines for a good price! Get your sardines here!" the salesman called out. Gon ran over.

"I'll buy some sardines," Yasuke's wife said from her back door. The sardine salesman left his cart piled up with sardines at the side of the road and went into Yasuke's house holding a couple of shiny sardines.

Gon reached into the cart and grabbed five or six sardines from the basket. He ran back to Hyōju's house, threw the sardines through Hyōju's back door, and ran back to his nest. As he glanced back from the top of the hill, he could see Hyōju in the distance still washing barley at the well.

Gon thought his good deed would make up for taking the eel.

The next day, Gon went into the mountains and gathered a bunch of chestnuts and carried them to Hyōju's house. When he peered in through the back door, he saw that Hyōju, who had only eaten part of his lunch, was sitting deep in thought, holding his dish in his hand. The strange thing was that Hyōju had a bruise on the side of his face. As Gon was wondering what had happened, Hyōju grumbled to himself, "I wonder who would throw sardines into my house. And now the sardine salesman thinks I'm a thief!"

Gon felt terrible. Poor Hyōju had been punched by the sardine salesman and got a terrible bruise on his face. Gon quietly crept toward the storeroom and left the chestnuts by the door.

The next day and the day after that, Gon gathered more chestnuts and brought them to Hyōju's house. And the following day, he also brought two or three mushrooms.

4

It was a lovely moonlit evening. Gon had just wandered past Nakayama Castle when he heard someone coming down the narrow path. Someone was speaking. The crickets were chirping.

Gon hid quietly by the side of the road. Voices drew closer and closer. It was Hyōju and a farmer named Kasuke.

"Hey, Kasuke," Hyōju said.

"Yeah?" Kasuke said.

"Something really strange has been happening lately."

"What?"

"Since my mother died, someone—I don't know who—has been bringing me chestnuts and mushrooms every day."

"Hmm, who could it be?"

"I don't know. They are left while I'm not looking."

Gon followed after them.

"Are you kidding?" Kasuke said.

"It's true. If you think I'm lying, then come see for yourself tomorrow. I'll show you the chestnuts."

"Wow, that's really strange."

Then the two men walked along in silence. Kasuke turned and looked behind him. Kasuke did not see Gon, who shrank back into the shadows, and they continued walking. When the two men came to Kichibē the farmer's house, they went inside. The sound of a Buddhist drum drifted out of the house. The shadow of a monk's head was visible through the window.

"They're going to say a prayer," thought Gon as he crouched near a well.

After a little while three more people came along and went into Kichibē's house. Someone was reading a prayer.

5

Gon stayed crouched by the well until the prayer was finished. Hyōju and Kasuke came out together and headed home. Gon followed them to listen to what they would say. He stayed close behind Hyōju.

When the two men reached the front of the castle, Kasuke said, "The gods must be looking down upon you."

"What do you mean?" Hyōju asked with surprise.

"I've been thinking about it, and I think that the gods have taken pity on you because you are all alone and have left you gifts."

"Do you really think so?"

"I really think so. So you should thank the gods every day in your prayers."

"I will," Hyōju said.

Gon thought that this was very unfair. "I'm the one who brings him chestnuts and mushrooms but instead of thanking me he is going to thank the gods. That's not fair," he thought.

6

The next day, Gon headed for Hyōju's house with a bunch of chestnuts. Hyōju was outside weaving rope. Gon snuck into the house through the back door.

Just at that moment, Hyōju looked up. He saw a fox go into his house. "That rotten Gon, the fox who stole my eel, is up to no good again," he thought.

"All right then," Hyōju said as he took his gun out from the shed and loaded it. Hyōju then tiptoed into the house, took aim at Gon, and shot him as he was sneaking out the front door. Gon toppled over and Hyōju came running. When Hyōju looked around the living room he saw a pile of chestnuts.

"Oh, no!" Hyōju said with surprise as he looked down at Gon. "Gon, it was you. The one who kept bringing me chestnuts," he said.

Gon just nodded with his eyes shut tight. Hyōju dropped his gun on the floor. A thin wisp of smoke floated out of the barrel.

EVENING CRANE

Kinoshita Junji

Characters:
YOHYŌ
TSŪ
SŌDO
UNZU
CHILDREN

Setting: A shabby house in the middle of a vast snow-covered landscape. Behind the house, the sun is setting, the sky is brilliant red.

(In the distance, the sound of children's voices singing a nursery rhyme is heard.)

> *The cloth that clothes the old man*
> *The cloth that clothes the old woman*
> *Chinkara kankara tontonton*

(YOHYŌ *is dozing by the stove inside the house. The singing stops and the children come running onstage.*)

CHILDREN: (*All together, as if singing.*) Lady, lady, sing us a song! Lady, lady, come play with us! Lady, lady, sing us a song!

YOHYŌ: (*Wakes up.*) What's going on? What's going on?

CHILDREN: Lady, let's play! Lady, sing us a song! Lady! Lady!

YOHYŌ: Are you looking for Tsū? Tsū's not here.

CHILDREN: She's not here? Really? No way! Where did she go?

YOHYŌ: I don't know where she went.

CHILDREN: Where did she go? When will she be back? Tell us, tell us, Mr. Yohyō.

YOHYŌ: Be quiet! (*He stands.*)

CHILDREN: (*Running away.*) Hey, hey, Mr. Yohyō is getting angry! Yohyō! Yohyō! Stupid Mr. Yohyō!

YOHYŌ: Heh-heh. Don't run away. Don't run away. I'll play with you.

CHILDREN: What shall we play?

YOHYŌ: What shall we play?

CHILDREN: The peg game.

YOHYŌ: OK. Let's play the peg game.

CHILDREN: Let's sing.

YOHYŌ: OK. Let's sing.

CHILDREN: Let's have a snowball fight.

YOHYŌ: OK. A snowball fight. (YOHYŌ *enters the circle of children as he says this.*)

CHILDREN: Let's play bird in the basket.

YOHYŌ: OK. Bird in the basket.

CHILDREN: Let's play deer, deer, how many horns.

YOHYŌ: OK. Deer, deer, how many horns. OK, here we go.

CHILDREN: Deer, deer, how many horns. (*They repeat this as they run away.*)

YOHYŌ: (*Running after them.*) Oh, I forgot! It would be terrible if Tsū came home and the soup were cold. My precious, precious Tsū. (*He goes inside and puts the pot on the stove.*)

(*Tsū comes out from the back of the house.*)

TSŪ: Hello dear.

YOHYŌ: Tsū, where were you?

TSŪ: Well, um, let's see. . . . What have you been up to?

YOHYŌ: Heh-heh. I didn't want the soup to be cold when you came back so I put it on the stove for you. Heh-heh.

TSŪ: Oh, thank you. Shall I start making dinner?

YOHYŌ: OK. I'll go play with the children. We're going to play the peg game.

TSŪ: Oh, my. The peg game.

YOHYŌ: And then we're going to have a snowball fight. And then we're going to sing.

TSŪ: And then . . . bird in the basket. And then deer, deer, how many horns. Right?

YOHYŌ: Yes. Deer, deer how many horns. Why don't you come along too, Tsū?

TSŪ: I'd like to. But I have to make dinner. . . .

YOHYŌ: Oh, that's OK. Come on. (*He pulls her along.*)

TSŪ: I can't.

YOHYŌ: I said come, so come. Come play with us.

TSŪ: I can't. I can't. I said I can't. (*She is laughing as she gets pulled along.*)

(*A nursery rhyme is heard in the distance.* SŌDO *and* UNZU *appear.*)

SŌDO: Her? That woman is Yohyō's wife?

UNZU: Yes. That Yohyō, all of a sudden he has a good wife and now he's so happy. Lately, all he does is sleep by the fire.

SŌDO: Like the stupid fool that he is, he used to be quite a hard worker. Why would a good woman like that go for a fool like him?

UNZU: She just appeared one day. And now he's living it up.

SŌDO: Hey, Unzu, you were lying, right? About the cloth?

UNZU: Nope, it's the truth. If I take it to the city, I can always get ten ryō for it.

SŌDO: Hmm. And you say that his wife weaves it?

UNZU: That's right. But she says that nobody can watch her weave, that no one can come into the weaving room. And Yohyō, being the honest person that he is, doesn't look in, and goes to sleep, and in the morning, the cloth is done. And it is beautiful cloth indeed.

SŌDO: It's called *Senbaori*?

UNZU: The people in the city call it that. Supposedly it is so hard to find that you'd usually have to go to India to get it.

SŌDO: Unzu, if you're the dealer, aren't you making a lot of money?

UNZU: Er, not all that much. . . .

SŌDO: Yeah, sure. But if it's real Senbaori then it must be worth fifty or a hundred ryō.

UNZU: You think so? What is it exactly? What is Senbaori?

SŌDO: It's cloth that's been woven from a thousand feathers plucked from a live crane.

UNZU: Really? And where do you think that woman gets all those crane feathers?

SŌDO: So, this is the weaving room. (*He wanders into the house and looks into the next room.*) So he's got a weaving room set up. Oh—

UNZU: What? What?

SŌDO: Look at this. Crane feathers. So, it's—

UNZU: —the real thing?

(*Pause.*)

(*Tsū, who has returned without being noticed, comes out from the back of the house.*)

UNZU: Yikes.

SŌDO: I'm, I'm sorry to intrude while you were out. . . .

(TSŪ *tilts her head to the side like a bird and looks at the two men inquisitively.*)

UNZU: Um, I'm Unzu from the next town over there, um, the one who sells the cloth.

(TSŪ *is silent.*)

SŌDO: Ma'am, he told me about the cloth. I'm also from the next town, my name is Sōdo, and I wanted to know something. Excuse me for asking, but is it real Senbaori?

(TSŪ *looks at them suspiciously, and then, as if she hears something, she quickly turns around and disappears into the back of the house.*)

(SŌDO *and* UNZU *look at each other quizzically.*)

SŌDO: Hey. . . .

UNZU: What? I don't think she understood what we were saying.

SŌDO: Yeah. She never seems to understand anything. And she acts like a bird.

UNZU: You're right. She's just like a bird.

(*Pause.*)

(*It grows dark and only the red flame of the stove is visible.*)

SŌDO: (*Looking at a crane feather.*) Hey, I've heard that cranes and snakes sometimes turn into humans.

UNZU: What?!

SŌDO: Yeah, . . . Come to think of it, yesterday Ninji was telling me that four or five days ago, in the evening, he was walking by the lake up in the mountains and saw a woman standing all alone by the water. He thought this was strange, and watched her, and as soon as she got into the water he said she turned into a crane.

UNZU: No!

SŌDO: And he said that the crane played in the water for a while and then turned back into a woman and went away.

UNZU: Waaaaaaa!!! (*He runs outside.*)

SŌDO: Hey, hey, stop making those strange noises. (*He wanders outside.*)

UNZU: So, so, that means that the woman is, is a crane. . . .

SŌDO: Don't be stupid. We don't know that. Hey, it was just a silly story.

UNZU: Oh, no, what have I done? I cheated Yohyō by making a lot of money for myself!

SŌDO: What are you worrying about? If it's real Senbaori, bring it to the city and you get a thousand ryō for it.

UNZU: Wha-huh? A thousand ryō?

SŌDO: And from what you said, that idiot Yohyō seems pretty greedy, and he is no idiot when it comes to money.

UNZU: Well, I suppose so, but. . . .

SŌDO: So you've got to get Yohyō on your side and get him to get his wife to weave more and more cloth.

UNZU: Well, um, I guess so. . . .

SŌDO: Hey, he's coming.

YOHYŌ: (*Wanders onstage.*) *The cloth that clothes the old woman, chinkarakankaratontonton.* . . . Oh, my, I completely forgot to make dinner for Tsū.

SŌDO: Hey, Yohyō.

YOHYŌ: Huh?

SŌDO: Remember me? It's Sōdo from the next village. . . . Unzu, tell him who I am.

YOHYŌ: Oh, Unzu, are you here about our business again?

UNZU: If you get me some more of that cloth I can make you a lot of money.

YOHYŌ: I don't have any more cloth.

SŌDO: Why not?

YOHYŌ: Tsū said that she's not making any more.

UNZU: Oh, no. But I can make you lots more money.

YOHYŌ: Hmmm, but I love my Tsū so much.

SŌDO: You love her? But if you get her to weave lots more cloth, you can make more money.

YOHYŌ: But whenever Tsū weaves the cloth she gets so skinny.

SŌDO: What do you mean, she gets skinny? Hey, Yohyō, just how did you meet your wife?

YOHYŌ: Huh? You mean Tsū? I can't remember exactly when, but one evening, as I was getting ready for bed, she came in and asked if I would make her my wife. Heh-heh.

SŌDO: Hmmm, by any chance, have you done anything to help a crane lately?

YOHYŌ: What? A crane? Yes, well I can't remember exactly when, but one day I was working in the fields when a crane that had been shot by an arrow landed nearby and I pulled out the arrow.

SŌDO: What? . . . Hmm. . . . Hey, Unzu, . . . It's sounding more and more as if it's true.

(UNZU *is shaking.*)

SŌDO: And if it's true, then I can make a whole lot of money. Hey, Yohyō, about that—that cloth. Unzu, you talk to him.

UNZU: Um, that, uh, if I brought that cloth to the city, I could get a thou—

SŌDO: Stupid. Listen, Yohyō, this time you could get hundreds of ryō, so couldn't you get her to make some more?

YOHYŌ: Hundreds? Really?

SŌDO: That's right. Hundreds. (*To* UNZU.) Right?

UNZU: That—that's right. You could make hundreds of ryō.

YOHYŌ: Oh, hundreds of ryō. . . .

SŌDO: Listen, Yohyō, you've got to speak to your wife again. (*He suddenly realizes that Tsū is watching them from inside the house.*) Come over here and I'll explain it to you in detail. (*He pulls* YOHYŌ *into the shadows.*)

(UNZU *follows along.* TSŪ *comes out of the house and watches them. She has a worried look on her face. The children come running.*)

CHILDREN: (*All together.*) Hey, the lady's here. Lady, let's play. Why did you run away? Lady, let's sing. Bird in the basket. Hide and go seek. Let's sing songs. Let's make a circle. (*They encirle her.*) Hey, hey, lady, hey.

TSŪ: Listen, it's already getting dark. That's all for today.

CHILDREN: No! Let's play. Come on, lady, let's sing a song.

TSŪ: (*In a faint voice.*) A song?

CHILDREN: Hide and go seek.

TSŪ: Hide and go seek?

CHILDREN: Make a circle.

TSŪ: Make a circle?

CHILDREN: Bird in the basket.

TSŪ: Bird in the basket?

CHILDREN: Bird in the basket. (*They make a circle around* TSŪ *and begin to walk around.*)

> *Basket, basket.*
> *The bird is in the basket.*
> *When will it come out?*
> *In the evening or the dawn*
> *The crane slides.*
> *Who is behind you? Who is behind you?*

Hey, lady, hey. Will you play hide and go seek with us? Will you close your eyes? Come on, lady.

TSŪ: (*She remains standing as she daydreams.*) What? Oh, all right. (*She crouches down and covers her eyes.*)

(*The children continue singing as they walk around in a circle. The stage becomes dark, and only TSŪ remains in a ring of light.*)

TSŪ: Yohyō, my precious Yohyō. What's happened to you? You're changing. I don't understand why, but you're becoming a stranger to me. You're becoming one of those people who speak in words I do not even understand, those people who once shot an arrow into me. You're becoming one of those horrible people. What's happened? What's happened to you? What should I do? What can I do? I don't know what to do. You saved my life. You didn't want anything in return. You felt sorry for me so you pulled out the arrow. I was so grateful. I came to you. And when I made you that cloth, you were as happy as a little child. That's why I endured the pain to weave you more and more cloth. And each time, you went and traded it for that thing you call "money." Even so, it's OK with me, if "money" is what makes you happy. But now you have plenty of "money," so now let's just the two of us live a quiet happy life in this little house. You are different from other people. You are a person of my world. That's why I planned on making a world with you in the middle of this big field and living with you forever—tending the land and playing with the children. But now you are moving away from me. You are getting further and further away. What am I to do? What am I to do?

(*The singing fades out during this monologue. It becomes light. The stage is empty except for TSŪ. TSŪ looks off stage and then runs into the house as if she is being chased. SŌDO, UNZU, and YOHYŌ appear.*)

SŌDO: So, you see? You scare her by telling her that if she doesn't weave the cloth you will leave her.

YOHYŌ: Heh-heh. That cloth. It's beautiful cloth, isn't it? Tsū wove it herself.

SŌDO: And not only is it beautiful cloth, but I can sell it for two or three times as much money as before. Do you understand? I can sell it for two or three times as much money. Try explaining it like that to your wife.

YOHYŌ: You're going to sell it for two or three times as much, right?

SŌDO: That's right. For hundreds of ryō.

YOHYŌ: Hundreds of ryō, right?

SŌDO: That's right. So you must make her weave it right away, right Unzu?

UNZU: Yes, that's right. Make her weave it tonight.

YOHYŌ: Hmm, but Tsū already said that she wouldn't weave any more.

SŌDO: Don't be an idiot! If it sells for a high price and you make a lot of money, then your wife will be thrilled. I guarantee it.

UNZU: He's right. She'll be thrilled.

YOHYŌ: Hmm. . . .

SŌDO: And on top of that, you'll get to see the city. The city is an amazing place, isn't it, Unzu?

UNZU: It sure is. It's an amazing place.

YOHYŌ: I bet the city is a mighty fine place.

SŌDO: That's right. All right then? So, not only will you make lots of money, but you'll get to see the city. When we go to the city, like we were just saying, we'll show you lots of interesting things. Or would you rather not go to the city?

YOHYŌ: No, no, I want to go.

UNZU: And you want to make lots of money, right?

YOHYŌ: Yes, I want to make money too.

SŌDO: (*Notices* TSŪ *inside the house.*) So, go inside then. Make her weave it right now. If she says she won't do it, tell her you're going to leave her.

YOHYŌ: . . . OK.

SŌDO: That's it, you can do it. (*He pushes* YOHYŌ *inside the house.*) OK now, Unzu, let's hide and watch what happens.

(SŌDO *and* UNZU *hide.*)

TSŪ: (*As soon as* SŌDO *and* UNZU *go away, she approaches* YOHYŌ *anxiously.*) Come on, dear, hurry up and come inside. You're soaked, you'll catch cold. Dinner is ready. You put the soup on the stove so it's nice and hot. So come inside. Come closer to the fire. Please.

YOHYŌ: Umm. . . .

TSŪ: Now, eat your dinner.

YOHYŌ: Hmm. . . . (*He eats.*)

TSŪ: What's the matter? Why are you so tired? You really shouldn't stay out so late when it's this cold. Don't run off anywhere else, OK? And don't you go talking with any more strangers, OK? OK?

YOHYŌ: Hmm. . . .

TSŪ: Promise me, OK? If you promise, I'll do anything you like. I'll do anything you like. You already have all that "money" that you like so much.

YOHYŌ: Yes. I do have money. I have lots of it. I put it in this bag.

TSŪ: That's right. So from now on let's just live here happily, just the two of us, OK? OK?

YOHYŌ: Yes. I love you, Tsū.

TSŪ: And I love you very much. And I want you to stay just the way you are, forever, OK?

YOHYŌ: Yes. I really love you, Tsū.

(*Pause.*)

TSŪ: Do you want some more? What's wrong? Don't you want any more? Huh?

YOHYŌ: Um, listen, Tsū. . . .

TSŪ: What?

YOHYŌ: You've done lots of things, right? You've seen the city.

TSŪ: Yes, but only from the sky—. (*She stops in midsentence.*) What's wrong? Don't you want any more dinner?

YOHYŌ: Umm. . . . (*He hesitates.*) Listen, Tsū. . . .

TSŪ: Hmm?

YOHYŌ: Listen, heh-heh! Oh, I can't say it.

TSŪ: Well, what is it? What's wrong?

YOHŌY: Well, it's like this. Oh, I can't say it!

TSŪ: But why? What can't you say? Should I try to guess?

YOHYŌ: Yes.

TSŪ: Let's see, do you want me to make more dumplings?

YOHYŌ: No, it's something else.

TSŪ: Well then, do you want me to sing a song? That's it, isn't it?

YOHYŌ: No, that's not it. I do like your singing. Not today, though.

TSŪ: What, I'm wrong again? Well then, do you want me to tell you stories about the city again? That's it, isn't it? See? I guessed right!

YOHYŌ: Umm, you're sort of wrong. But you're sort of right.

TSŪ: Sort of wrong and sort of right? What is it? Tell me.

YOHYŌ: Do you promise you won't get mad?

TSŪ: Now, why would I ever get mad at you? What is it? Tell me please.

YOHYŌ: Well, um, it's like this, I want to go to the city.

TSŪ: What?

YOHYŌ: I'm going to go to the city and make lots and lots of money. And, heh-heh, I want some more of that cloth again. . . .

TSŪ: (*She is shocked.*) That cloth? But, I told you. . . .

YOHYŌ: (*He changes his mind.*) Never mind. I don't want it. I don't want it.

TSŪ: (*To herself.*) That cloth. He promised. I told him it was the last time. . . .

YOHYŌ: Yes, you did say so. And I don't want it any more. I don't want it. (*Like a child who has been chastised, he tries very hard to keep from crying.*)

TSŪ: (*Alarmed.*) Those people. Those people who were here just now. I knew it. Those people are pulling you toward the other side.

YOHYŌ: What? Don't be angry, Tsū. . . .

(TSŪ *is silent.*)

YOHYŌ: Hey, Tsū. . . .

TSŪ: (*To no one in particular.*) Money. . . . Money. . . . Money. . . . Why does he want it so badly?

YOHYŌ: Look, if we have money we can buy the good things.

TSŪ: Buy? What does "buy" mean? What does "the good things" mean? What else do you want beside me? No, no. I don't want you to want anything else but me. I don't want money. I don't want to buy things. All I want is for you to love me. And I don't want anything else but for the two of us to go on living here together forever.

YOHYŌ: Right, I like being with you, just the two of us. I really love you, Tsū.

TSŪ: Yes. Yes. Yes. (*She hugs* YOHYŌ.) So lets stay this way forever. Don't go away. Don't ever leave me and go away.

YOHYŌ: Don't be silly. Why would I ever go away? Silly. Silly. Silly.

TSŪ: When we're sitting here and you're holding me like this it makes me think of that time. . . . Through the vast sky, innocently, without a thought in my head. . . . It makes me feel the way I did back then. . . . I'm content like this. I am content if only I am with you. Let's stay together forever, OK? Don't go away somewhere far away, OK? (*She pauses and then suddenly pushes* YOHYŌ *away.*) You, you're still thinking about the city. You're thinking about "money."

YOHYŌ: Hey, hey, what, what's gotten into you?

TSŪ: You are. I knew it, you are. . . . (*She suddenly becomes angry.*) No. No. No. I don't want you to go to the city. You'll never come back. You'll never come back to me.

YOHYŌ: Hey, I'll come back. I'll come back. I'll go to the city and make lots and lots of money. We'll go to the city together.

(*Pause.*)

TSŪ: Do you really want to go to the city that badly? Do you really want "money" that badly?

YOHYŌ: Well of course, everyone wants money.

TSŪ: Do you want it that badly? Do you want to go that badly? You love money more than you love me? And the city too? Is that it?

YOHYŌ: If you put it that way, then I don't like it.

TSŪ: What do you mean? You don't like it?

YOHYŌ: I don't like it. I don't like it. And I don't like you. You're mean to me.

TSŪ: Well, then. . . .

YOHYŌ: Weave the cloth. I'm going to the city. I'm going to make money.

TSŪ: You're a horrible person. A horrible person. How dare you say that to me. How dare you. . . .

(YOHYŌ *is silent.*)

TSŪ: Hey! Hey! Hey! (*She grabs* YOHYŌ*'s shoulders and shakes him.*) Do you mean it? Darling, is that really how you feel?

YOHYŌ: I'll leave you if you don't weave the cloth.

TSŪ: Oh!

YOHYŌ: Weave the cloth. Right now. They say that they can sell it for two or three times as much this time. Hundreds of ryō.

TSŪ: (*She is suddenly very surprised and confused.*) What? What?

What did you say? Just now. You said, "Weave the cloth, right now," and then what did you say?

YOHYŌ: I said hundreds of ryō. They said that they can sell it for two or three times as much this time.

(TSŪ *tilts her head like a bird and looks at* YOHYŌ *questioningly.*)

YOHYŌ: You see, this time, you see, they can sell it for two or three times as much as before.

TSŪ: (*Screams.*) I don't understand. I can't understand anything you're saying. It's the same as with those people from before. I only see your mouth moving. I only hear your voice. But what you are saying. . . . You, you, in the end you too are speaking the words of those people, words of a world I do not understand. What am I to do? What am I to do? What am I to do?

YOHYŌ: Hey, what's wrong? Tsū. . . .

TSŪ: What's wrong, Tsū? What? Is that what you said? You said, "What's wrong, Tsū?" Right? Just now.

(YOHYŌ *is startled and stares at* TSŪ.)

TSŪ: What? Am I wrong? You said something else? Huh? Huh? You are moving farther and farther away. You're moving farther away. You're getting smaller. What, what can I do? What? (*She goes outside.*) Stop it. Stop it. Stop pulling Yohyō away. Please. Please. Please. Where are you two? Please. I beg you. Please do not pull my Yohyō away. Please, please. I beg you. I beg you. Are you there? Are you hiding? Come out, traitors. It's not fair. Hey! Hey! You are horrible. . . . My Yohyō. . . Why don't you come out? Come out! No, no, no, I'm sorry, to say you're horrible. I beg you, please. Please. Please. (*She gets weaker and weaker and falls into the snow.*)

YOHYŌ: (*He comes out of the house frightened.*) Hey, what's wrong? Tsū. . . . (*He holds her.*)

TSŪ: (*She wakes up.*) Ah, my darling. . . .

YOHYŌ: Now, come back inside the house. You must be cold in the snow. . . . (*He pulls her to the fire.*)

(TSŪ *and* YOHYŌ *sit silently for a while.*)

TSŪ: Do you really want to go to the city that badly?

YOHYŌ: Well, umm, heh-heh. . . .

(*Pause.*)

YOHYŌ: I hear that the city is beautiful. They say that the cherry blossoms are in bloom now.

(*Pause.*)

YOHYŌ: And you said there were cows that pull carts with people on them, and that there are lots of them walking around. That's what you told me, Tsū.

(*Pause.*)

YOHYŌ: Oh, I'm so sleepy. (*He rolls over onto his back.*)

(*Pause.*)

(TSŪ *covers* YOHYŌ. *She watches him sleep intently. Then she gets up quickly and gets a cloth bag from the corner of the room. She reaches inside and pulls out some coins. The coins fall from her hand to the ground. She stares at them. The stage suddenly grows dark. Only Tsū and the shining coins remain in a pool of light.*)

TSŪ: It's because of this. Everything has happened because of it. Money. Money. I just wanted him to see the beautiful cloth. It made me so happy when he saw it. That is the only reason why I risked my life to weave it for him. And now it's the only way I can keep him with me. Weave the cloth so he can have money. If I don't, then . . . If I don't, then he will leave me. But, . . . but it's OK, if money . . . if having lots of money makes you that happy. . . . If you want to go to the city that badly, . . . and if this is what I have to do to keep you from leaving me, . . . I will weave you one more piece of that cloth. And then you will have to forgive me, because once I have done it I may die. Take the cloth and go to the city and make lots of money. But come back, you must come back. You just have to. And this time you must stay with me, and the two of us will live together forever. . . .

(*It becomes light.*)

TSŪ: (TSŪ *shakes* YOHYŌ *until he wakes up.*) Yohyō, Yohyō. . . .

YOHYŌ: Huh?

TSŪ: Listen, . . . I'm going to weave the cloth for you.

YOHYŌ: Huh? What are you saying?

TSŪ: I'm going to weave the cloth for you.

YOHYŌ: Really, the cloth? You're going to weave it for me? But Tsū. . . .

TSŪ: Yes, I'm going to weave it for you, just one more piece.

YOHYŌ: Do you mean it? Well, I. . . .

TSŪ: Yes. I'm really going to weave it for you. And I want you to take it and go to the city.

YOHYŌ: Really? It's OK if I go to the city? Really? Well, I. . . .

TSŪ: Yes. And you must bring back lots of that money you like so much. And then . . . and then. . . .

YOHYŌ: You're going to weave it for me. And I can take it to the city. Yes, I will make lots of money and bring it back. Yes, I will make lots and lots of money. I will.

TSŪ: (*She stares at the overjoyed* YOHYŌ.) All right, then, just this once. And you must promise me, as you always do. You must never look in while I am weaving. OK? Promise.

YOHYŌ: Right, I must never look in. OK, I understand. So, you're going to weave the cloth for me.

TSŪ: I beg you. You must really promise never to look in. If you look in, it's all over between us.

YOHYŌ: Yes. Yes. I promise. Yes. I'll take it to the city. I will sell it for two or three times as much as before.

TSŪ: You must promise. You must promise not to look. (*She enters the weaving room.*)

(*The sound of the loom can be heard.* SŌDO *comes dashing out of the shadows.* UNZU *follows.*)

SŌDO: We did it, Unzu. She's started weaving.

UNZU: When we were watching from over there, I couldn't help but feel sorry for that woman. . . .

SŌDO: Don't be an idiot. We're all about to make lots of money. There's no point feeling sorry for her. (*He goes into the house and tries to peek into the weaving room.*)

YOHYŌ: Hey, don't do that. You're not allowed to look in.

UNZU: Hey, Sōdo, he says that we can't look while she's weaving.

SŌDO: Pay no attention to him. If we don't look while she's weaving, how will we know if it's real Senbaori?

YOHYŌ: No, don't. You can't. She'll get angry. Stop!

UNZU: Hey, Sōdo. . . .

SŌDO: Let go of me! Let go! (*He looks in.*) Oh, my!

UNZU: What, what's wrong?

SŌDO: Oh, you've got to see this. It's a crane. It's a crane. A crane is weaving on the loom.

UNZU: Wha—what? A crane? (*He looks in.*) Oh, it's a c—c—crane. The woman is gone, and there's a crane in there. It's plucking its own feathers and then running back and forth over the loom.

SŌDO: Hey, Unzu, now we know it's true.

UNZU: Yeah. . . .

YOHYŌ: What? What's going on?

SŌDO: Your true love is in there. Come on, Unzu, we'll have the cloth in our hands by tomorrow morning. Let's go home and wait.

UNZU: O—OK.

YOHYŌ: Hey, what's in there? What's going on in there? Tsū's not there?

UNZU: (*Being dragged off by* SŌDO.) It's a c—c—crane. There's a crane in there!

(SŌDO *pulls* UNZU *away.*)

YOHYŌ: What? A crane? There's a crane in there? In here? Oh, I want to look. But I can't. I'm not allowed. I'm not allowed. Tsū will get mad at me. But what is the crane doing? Oh, I want to look. But I can't look, right? Hey, Tsū, hey, I'm just going to take a peek. OK. No, I can't, I can't. Tsū said that I absolutely cannot look. Hey, Tsū, hey, Tsū. Why don't you answer? Hey! Oh, she's not saying anything. I want to look. I want to look. All right, I'm just going to take a peek. (*He finally looks*) What's this? There's a crane in here. And Tsū's gone. What's happened to her? Hey, Tsū! Tsū! She's not there. What should I do? Tsū's not there. Tsū's not there. Tsū! Tsū! Tsū! Tsū! (*He looks around for Tsū and wanders outside.*)

(*The sound of the loom continues.*)

(*The lights on stage black out. As the sound of the loom continues in the background, we hear the following poem.*)

Yohyō, Yohyō, where are you going
Through dark snow-covered fields
With no one to guide you
You go looking for Tsū.
Tsū! Tsū!
Until your voice fails you,
The morning sun's rays soon shine on white snow
And into the afternoon.
Tsū! Tsū!
And in the evening
Behind the house is a sheet of red
The setting sun.

(*It becomes light. The sun is rising. The sound of the loom continues.* SŌDO and UNZU *are tending to* YOHYŌ, *whom they have carried back into the house.*)

UNZU: Hey, wake up, Yohyō.

SŌDO: What happened to you? You collapsed in the snow. What were you doing all the way out there?

UNZU: If we hadn't come along, you would have frozen to death by now.

YOHYŌ: Tsū . . . Tsū. . . .

UNZU: He's coming to. Hey, Yohyō.

SŌDO: Hey, Yohyō, get a hold of yourself.

YOHYŌ: Tsū! Tsū!

(*Pause*)

SŌDO: She's still in there weaving.

UNZU: Yeah. He told us that she always finishes by morning, but it's taking all night and all day.

SŌDO: Should we peek in again? (*He goes to the door.*)

The sound of the loom suddenly stops.

UNZU: It's st—stopped.

SŌDO: She's going to come out.

(*They rush outside and hide in the shadows.* TSŪ *comes out holding two pieces of cloth. She looks very thin.*)

TSŪ: Yohyō! Yohyō! (*She shakes* YOHYŌ *awake.*)

YOHYŌ: Tsū! Tsū!

TSŪ: Yohyō!

YOHYŌ: Yes, Tsū. (*He remembers.*) Oh, Tsū. (*He hugs* TSŪ *and begins to cry.*) Tsū! Tsū! Where were you Tsū? You were gone and I. . .

TSŪ: I'm sorry I made you wait so long. I've finished the cloth. Look. Look at the cloth.

YOHYŌ: Huh? . . . Oh, the cloth. Oh, so the cloth is done. Ohhhhh! . . .

(TSŪ *watches the delighted* YOHYŌ *intently.*)

YOHYŌ: Yes, this is quite splendid. It's beautiful. Oh, and there are two pieces. There are two pieces, aren't there?

TSŪ: Yes, Two pieces. That's why it took so long. Take them and go to the city.

YOHYŌ: Yes. I'll go to the city. And you'll come with me, won't you?

(TSŪ *is crying.*)

YOHYŌ: Hey, you'll come with me and we'll see the sights, right?

TSŪ: You, you looked in, didn't you?

YOHYŌ: Yes, I couldn't wait to see the city. Tsū, this is wonderful cloth.

TSŪ: But I begged you not to. I made you promise. Why? Why did you look?

YOHYŌ: What? Why are you crying?

TSŪ: I wanted to be with you forever and ever. Please keep one of these pieces of cloth. Will you keep it and treasure it? I put my heart and soul into weaving it for you.

YOHYŌ: Yes, you really did a wonderful job.

TSŪ: (*Taking hold of* YOHYŌ's *shoulders, she says firmly.*) Cherish it, do you hear? You must treasure it, OK?

YOHYŌ: (*Like a child.*) Yes, I will treasure it. I will do whatever you say. But, Tsū, won't you come with me to the city?

TSŪ: No, I. . . . (*She laughs and stands up. She becomes completely white.*) I've become too thin. I used all the feathers I could use. With what I have left, I can just barely fly. (*She laughs.*)

YOHYŌ: (*He suddenly senses that something is wrong.*) Hey, Tsū. (*He tries to hold on to her, but his hands only grasp the air.*)

TSŪ: Yohyō. Please take care of yourself. Have a long and healthy life.

(YOHYŌ *is silent. From far away, the children can be heard singing the nursery rhyme.*)

> *The cloth that clothes the old man*
> *The cloth that clothes the old woman*
> *Chinkara kankara tontonton*

TSŪ: Oh, I must say goodbye to the children too. How many times have I sung that song and played with them? Yohyō, please do not forget me. I will never forget you. We only had a very short time together, but I will never ever forget being wrapped in your pure, pure love and the days I spent singing and playing with the children. No matter where I go. . . .

YOHYŌ: But Tsū, . . . Where are you going?

TSŪ: Please do not forget me. Please keep one piece of that cloth and treasure it forever.

YOHYŌ: Wait, Tsū. . . .

TSŪ: Goodbye. Goodbye. . . .

YOHYŌ: Tsū, hey, wait! I said wait! I'm coming too.

TSŪ: You can't. You can't. I can no longer live in human form. I must return alone to the sky. Goodbye. Take care. Goodbye. Goodbye. Goodbye. . . . (*She disappears.*)

YOHYŌ: Tsū! Tsū! Tsū! Where did you go? Hey Tsū! Hey! Hey! Tsū! Tsū! (*He stumbles outside.*)

(SŌDO *and* UNZU *come running and hold him up.*)

UNZU: (*Panting. To* SŌDO) Hey. . . .

SŌDO: (*Panting.*) She dis—disapeared. . . .

(YOHYŌ *is unconscious in* UNZU's *arms. The children come running.*)

CHILDREN: (*In unison, as if singing.*) Lady, lady, let's sing. Lady, lady, let's play. Lady, lady, let's sing. . . .

(*Pause.*)

CHILDREN: The lady's not here? No way! (*To* YOHYŌ.) Hey, where did the lady go? When is she coming back? Hey, hey, Mr. Yohyō.

(*YOHYŌ is distraught. He goes back into his house.*)

YOHYŌ: Tsū! The children have come to play. They want you to sing with them. Hey, Tsū. . . .

(*Pause.*)

A CHILD: (*Suddenly points up into the sky.*) It's a crane. It's a crane. A crane is flying by.

SŌDO: A crane. . . .

UNZU: Ohhh. . . .

CHILDREN: A crane. A crane. A crane is flying by. (*They repeat this as they run after the crane.*)

UNZU: Hey, Yohyō, look, a crane. . . .

SŌDO: It's wobbling. . . .

(*Pause.*)

SŌDO: (*To no one in particular.*) Well, I'm glad she wove two pieces. (*He tries to take the two pieces of cloth out of* Yohyō'*s hands, but though Yohyō is unconscious, he will not let go.*)

UNZU: (*He picks up* YOHYŌ *in his arms, intently following the crane with his eyes.*) It's getting smaller and smaller. . . .

YOHYŌ: Tsū. . . . Tsū. . . . (*As if to follow the crane, Yohyō staggers one or two steps. Holding on tightly to the cloth, he stands still, looking up at the sky.*)

(SŌDO *also looks up. The three of them stare at a point far up in the sky. The faint sound of the nursery rhyme can be heard in the distance.*)

POEMS

CRADLE SONG

Kitahara Hakushū

The canary sings
the cradle song.
Sleep sleep, little baby,
sleep.

The loquat sways
above the cradle.
Sleep sleep, little baby,
sleep.

The squirrel swings on
the cradle rope.
Sleep sleep, little baby,
sleep.

The yellow moon shines
upon the cradle's dreams.
Sleep sleep, little baby,
sleep.

THIS ROAD

Kitahara Hakushū

This road is a road I've been down before,
Oh yes, I remember,
The acacia are in bloom.

That hill is a hill I've seen before,
Oh yes, I remember,
Look, it's the white clock tower!

This road is a road I've been down before,
Oh yes, I remember,
I came this way in a carriage with my mother!

That cloud is a cloud I've seen before,
Oh yes, I remember,
The hawthorn branches are drooping.

THE BLUE-EYED DOLL

Noguchi Ujō

This blue-eyed doll
made of celluloid
was born in America.

When she reached
the port of Japan
her eyes were full of tears.

"I can't understand
what people are saying.
What will happen
if I get lost?"

Sweet girls
of Japan
please be kind
and play with her.

RED SHOES

Noguchi Ujō

The girl
with red shoes
was taken away
by a foreigner

She boarded a ship
at Yokohama pier and
was taken away
by a foreigner

I suppose now
she has blue eyes
and lives
in the foreigner's land

Every time I see red shoes
I wonder what happened to her
Every time I meet a foreigner
I wonder what happened to her

CANARY

Saijo Yaso

The canary that forgot its song, shall I throw it away in the mountains ?

No, no you can't do that!

The canary that forgot its song, shall I whip it with a willow branch ?

No, no that would be cruel!

If we float the canary that forgot its song
in a boat made of ivory
with a silver oar on the moonlit sea
it will remember the song it forgot how to sing.

Yukie Ohta received her B.A. from Barnard College and her M.A. from The University of Chicago. She has been translating Japanese children's literature for the past ten years. She currently designs handbags and owns a boutique in Brooklyn, N.Y.

Joan E. Ericson was raised in Hiroshima Prefecture, Japan, and grew up listening to Japanese children's stories. Her publications include "The Origins of the Concept of Women's Literature" in *The Woman's Hand*, edited by P. Schalow and J. Walker (Stanford University Press, 1996) and *Be a Woman: Hayashi Fumiko and Modern Japanese Women's Literature* (University of Hawaii Press, 1997). Ericson is Associate Professor of Japanese at Colorado College where she teaches courses in Japanese literature, language, culture, and the history of childhood. She lives in Colorado Springs with her husband and two daughters.

Keico Watanabe is a New York–based painter, graphic designer, and illustrator. She has shown her work throughout Japan, Europe, and the United States and owns a graphic design firm in Tokyo.

www.ingramcontent.com/pod-product-compliance
Lightning Source LLC
Chambersburg PA
CBHW070541100726
47907CB00004B/1222

* 9 7 8 0 7 6 5 6 0 5 5 6 6 *